D3

Problem C____ ar QUIRKY KID?

A Commonsense Guide for Parents

How to Help Kids Who Don't Fit In,
Can't Get Along, Are Too Fearful,
Sad, Anxious, or Angry, and More . . .

Rita Sommers-Flanagan, Ph.D., John Sommers-Flanagan, Ph.D.

free spirit
PUBLiSHiNG®

Works
for kids®

Library of Congress Cataloging-in-Publication Data
Sommers-Flanagan, Rita, 1953–
    Problem child or quirky kid? : a commonsense guide / by Rita and John
        Sommers-Flanagan.
        p. cm.
    Includes bibliographical references and index.
    ISBN 1-57542-121-6
        1. Problem children. 2. Discipline of children. 3. Behavior disorders in children.
        I. Sommers-Flanagan, John, 1957– II. Title.

HQ773.S63 2002
649'.64—dc21   2002012333

At the time of this book's publication, all facts and figures cited are the most current available; all telephone numbers, addresses, and Web site URLs are accurate and active; all publications, organizations, Web sites, and other resources exist as described in this book; and all have been verified. The authors and Free Spirit Publishing make no warranty or guarantee concerning the information and materials given out by organizations or content found at Web sites, and we are not responsible for any changes that occur after this book's publication. If you find an error or believe that a resource listed here is not as described, please contact Free Spirit Publishing. Parents, teachers, and other adults: We strongly urge you to monitor children's use of the Internet.

Edited by Pat Samples
Cover by Percolator
Interior book design by Marieka Heinlen
Index compiled by Randl Ockey

10 9 8 7 6 5 4 3 2 1
Printed in the United States of America

Free Spirit Publishing Inc.
217 Fifth Avenue North, Suite 200
Minneapolis, MN 55401-1299
(612) 338-2068
help4kids@freespirit.com
www.freespirit.com

Dedication

To our own parents, who still find us quirky.

Acknowledgments

First, we'd like to thank the enthusiastic professionals at Free Spirit Publishing for approaching us with this excellent idea, and for all the ways they've enhanced the project. Our special thanks go to the president of Free Spirit, Judy Galbraith—a woman of heart, wisdom, and vision. Our editor, Pat Samples, devoted endless hours to the project. Her attention to detail and sensitivity to the issues parents face improved the manuscript considerably. We are grateful to our professional settings, Families First and the University of Montana, for being places that support our writing. And finally, we couldn't write a book like this if we hadn't had a chance to "walk the walk." We'd like to thank our daughters, Chelsea and Rylee, for living life so fully, joyously, and openly, and for helping teach us how to be better parents.

Contents

Introduction

Most of the parents we know have lots of questions about their children. They especially wonder what's normal and what's not, and how they should handle the problems they're having with their children.

You probably picked up this book because you've got concerns like this about your child. Perhaps your situation is similar to ones we've heard about in our parenting classes:

I'm at the end of my rope. My daughter won't take her bath. She won't go to bed. And, she won't get up in the morning and refuses to go to school. It's driving me crazy. This can't be normal. What can I do?

※ ♪♪♪♪♪ ♪ ♪♪ ■

It seems like my son has no conscience. He hurts our cat and he gets in fights at school. His teacher's ready to kick him out of class. Should I take him to a counselor? Should he be on some sort of medication?

※ ♪♪♪♪♪ ♪ ♪♪ ■

My son is four and he's still wetting the bed. My daughter is two years old and she's already potty trained. What's wrong with him? Does he need to see a doctor?

※ ♪♪♪♪♪ ♪ ♪♪ ■

It happens almost every night. Around midnight or one in the morning, my five-year-old wakes up with a blood-curdling scream. But then when we rush into her room, she doesn't really seem awake and we can't console her. What should we do?

※ ♪♪♪♪♪ ♪ ♪♪ ■

Not only have we heard plenty of stories like these over the years, we've had plenty of tough times ourselves as parents. We remember worrying about both our daughters when they were younger—wondering whether the heaving sobs, the blood-curdling screams in the night, or the insistence that dragons are real were signs of big problems or just part of a normal childhood.

What we've discovered in our experiences as parents, therapists, and teachers is that while good parenting takes love, it also takes more than that. Parents need lots of courage and a willingness to learn things and try new ideas. We want to thank you for seeking out resources such as this book to help you better understand your child. Doing so is a sign of your deep love and concern as a parent. It's also a sign of great courage. We applaud you for being willing to explore whether or not your child has a serious problem. Reading this book will help you understand your child's behavior better and make it easier for you to determine if this behavior is normal or not, and what to do about it.

As you read and think about the possible problems your child might have, your courage and patience may be tested. That's because figuring out whether your child is mostly normal, or a bit quirky, or in need of professional help—the primary focus of this book—can be complex and sometimes confusing. We'll do our best to help you sort it out. While we can't promise you a Ph.D. in parenting from reading this book, you will get important information about your child's problems, advice on how you can help at home, and useful tips on how to get further help if you need it.

You Might Be Glad Your Child *Isn't* Normal

We recently told some friends we were writing a book. "How nice," one of them said. "What's it about?"

"We're writing it for parents who are worried if their child is normal," we answered.

One person in the group scowled and responded, "Well, I've always been glad mine *aren't normal.*"

This comment is a reminder that *normal* is a loaded word. He was reacting to the notion of normal meaning as a prescribed sameness. The extreme (and, we think, spooky) example of this meaning could come through human genetic engineering, potentially allowing parents to choose the height, weight, eye color, intellect, and even disposition of their children! Our friend's point was this: Isn't it better if our kids can just be their quirky little selves and not have to constantly mold themselves to fit some preset norm? Of course, we heartily agree with his point. However, as we all know, there are times when a child's behavior can get a little too unusual or troublesome, which is exactly why we've written this book. In such cases, it's important to understand if a child's actions are more or less normal, or whether the child needs significant help in order to achieve good mental health and to live well.

We'll define more completely what we mean by "normal" and "abnormal" in Chapter 1, but for now, keep these basic definitions in mind. A normal child is able to play and do schoolwork without major problems. Normal children don't stand out too much in a crowd (at least not in ways that make you or your child feel awful), and they basically function pretty well most of the time. In contrast, abnormal means unusual or deviant. Abnormal children are noticeable and often have trouble functioning in healthy ways. We recognize that we're oversimplifying these definitions for now, because as you probably know, many people are unusual—talented performers, for example—but do just fine when it comes to daily functioning. Again, you'll learn more on what's normal and what's not in Chapter 1.

How This Book Will Help You

Overall, this book is designed to help you if you're worried about your child's behaviors, attitudes, feelings, or general development. It's for parents or other adults caring for children who have trouble fitting in socially, are unhappy, or can't get along, or who seem overly anxious and fearful. We offer guidelines for figuring out whether your child's problems are serious. We also suggest home-based strategies for dealing with your child's problems and offer ideas about who to call or where to go if your child's behavior becomes disturbing or severe.

A Few Basic Beliefs

Some basic principles or beliefs underlie what we have to say in this book. Being familiar with them will help you get the most out of your reading.

Each Child Is Unique

We believe children have the right to be themselves and to live well-adjusted and happy lives whatever their special qualities and interests. We don't believe all children should behave the same way, feel the same about things, or fit into a tight, stereotypic way of being just to make parents, teachers, or neighbors happy. To put it simply, we like quirky kids!

Children Deserve Supportive Surroundings

We also believe your child has a right to healthy, nurturing home and school environments. If, for any reason, these basics aren't present, think about getting help to make sure they are.

A Professional Partner Can Help You When Your Child Is Hurting

You're the person who knows your child best, and in this book we'll suggest many things you can do to help your child with problem behaviors or feelings. But when you're not sure how serious these problems are, getting input and diagnostic impressions from a mental health professional is a smart move. While this book gives some clues about how a diagnosis is made, it isn't designed so that you will be able to officially "diagnose" your child. Instead, we have tried to give enough information to either reassure you that things aren't that bad, or to help you feel more confident in seeking professional assistance. A mental health professional has the special training needed to give diagnoses and can become an important partner with you in helping your child.

Seeking Help Is a Sign of Strength

Children develop problems for many reasons. Sometimes parents blame themselves, but in this book we encourage you to avoid doing that and instead focus on solutions. Parents are also sometimes reluctant to seek help outside of their family when their children have problems, but we believe that seeking help, when needed, is something to be proud of. We wish we could change public thinking so that getting needed help is viewed more widely as a sign of strength.

Early Help Can Prevent Bigger Problems

You don't need some diagnosable, big, giant, overwhelming problems to get help. In fact, sometimes, by getting help early, you avoid bigger trouble later.

What's in This Book, Chapter by Chapter

In Chapter 1, we talk about what's "normal." We describe nine unique temperaments that children are born with and give you some clues about how to distinguish a harmless temperamental quirk from behavior that is of more serious concern. The chapter also spells out how mental health professionals go about deciding if your child's troubling feelings or behaviors are abnormal and in need of attention.

Chapters 2 through 9 cover common childhood problems. These problems include: fears, worries, and anxious behaviors; body concerns; attention deficit hyperactivity disorder; childhood depression and mood troubles; sexual and social development; stress and trauma; oppositional/defiant behaviors; and serious troubles with conduct. Within each chapter, we provide examples, definitions, information on what's typical at different ages, and a few home-based remedies ("Helpful Hints") for parents to consider. These home-based tips can be helpful whether your child's behavior problems are serious enough to require professional help or are simply on the quirky side.

In Chapter 10, we briefly talk about difficulties that might be more rare and more serious, such as tendency toward violence, obsessive-compulsive disorder, and severe eating difficulties. These are troubles that may require a team of professionals for management and solutions.

Of course, your child is not likely to have all the problems described in Chapters 2–10, so you may find it helpful, after reading Chapter 1, to go directly to the chapter or chapters that seem to fit the problems that most concern you. You may find suggestions in those chapters to read other specific chapters if your child's problem behaviors fit more than one possible category or diagnosis.

In Chapter 11, we explain the complex and sometimes confusing world of mental health care and describe how you might get the help you need if your child's problems are serious. With all the professional titles and credentials that exist, parents often wonder "Who's who and what do they do?" That being the case, it's important to have a basic understanding of the different types of mental health care providers in order to choose the appropriate ones to call on for help.

Finally, in Chapter 12, you'll find a few ideas about how to get yourself and your child ready to go for professional help. This chapter includes a brief discussion of common theories and therapy techniques that mental health professionals use with children.

How to Use This Book

Depending on what you want to get out of this book, there are several ways you can approach reading it:

- If you want to get a broad understanding of a wide range of problems that your child might experience and some good ways to respond to each of them, you will benefit from reading the book cover to cover.

- If your child has a specific problem that seems to match the title of one of the "problem" chapters (Chapters 2–10), you can direct your attention primarily to that chapter. But we strongly recommend that you read Chapter 1 first to get an overview of children's temperaments and how to determine what's normal. We also suggest you read Chapters 11 and 12, which offer detailed guidance through the process of getting professional help.

- If you want to use the book just for a quick reference, you can review the three common lists in each of the specific problem chapters: "Serious Signs" that tell you whether the problem needs professional attention; "Helpful Hints" that offer tips for things you can try at home to help your child with a particular problem; and "Check It Out" that suggest books, videos, and Web sites with more information on the problem.

This Book Is About Your Child

This book is written to help you with any child in your care, such as your biological child, adopted child, stepchild, niece, nephew, or student. We talk about each of the various behavior problems in terms of what you might be noticing if your child has this problem and how you can respond to these problems in helpful ways.

For simpler reading, references to gender have been alternated by chapter. In odd-numbered chapters we use the pronoun "she." In even-numbered chapters, we use "he." You can change the pronoun in your mind to match your child's gender, if this is helpful.

You Can't Know It All

You can't possibly know everything about children's problems, and you can't necessarily be expected to "fix," heal, or change your child's deeply troubling behaviors on your own. But we encourage you to stay involved with your child, to know what's bugging him, what's hurting her, what's important to him, what's stupid and what's cool, what's embarrassing and what's overwhelming. Get help when it's needed. That's what this book is all about—providing you with the information you need to decide 1) when things can be worked through at home, 2) when your child is just being a bit quirky, but normal, and 3) when wisdom would say it's time to go get help for your child's sake.

Good luck and thanks for being a parent who cares enough to keep learning.

Rita Sommers-Flanagan & John Sommers-Flanagan

Chapter 1

What's Normal, What's Not?

Ribsy was a friendly dog. He followed
Henry and his friends to school. He kept the mail-
man company. He wagged his tail at the milkman, who always
stopped to pet him. People liked Ribsy, and Ribsy liked people.
Ribsy was what you might call a well-adjusted dog.
This did not mean that Ribsy had no troubles. He did have troubles,
and high on the list were fleas, particularly one mean hungry flea that
persistently nipped Ribsy right under his collar where he could not
get at it no matter how hard he scratched with his hind foot.
If it had not been for that flea, things might have been
different for Ribsy.

—**Beverly Cleary,** *Ribsy*

Like the friendly dog Ribsy, most children are generally well-adjusted. They handle ups and downs fairly well and get along with other people most of the time. Yet, no two children, not even genetically identical twins, are exactly alike. Your child has unique strengths, limits, and quirks. Those particular qualities of your child may delight you at times, and other times may challenge or disappoint you.

Helping your child grow up is a demanding job. Like most parents, you probably want your child to express her unique individuality. Yet you also want her, perhaps despite her particular quirks, to be well-adjusted and successful. The balance between treasuring her uniqueness and getting her to behave so she'll be able to enjoy a successful and fairly happy life isn't always easy.

Like most parents, you may be concerned about whether your child is developing normally—in a way that's more or less typical and free of major problems. You may wonder: Is my baby sitting up at the right age? When should she start talking and when should she start using sentences? Is this too early for her to be interested in boys? Fortunately, charts and guidelines exist to help you know if your child's physical development is below average, above average, or on target. Of course, in terms of positive attributes, most of us want our children to be like "all" the children public radio show host Garrison Keillor describes in the fictional town of Lake Wobegon— *above average!*

Whenever you have worries about whether your child's physical development is normal, you can readily turn to medical professionals for information. Most city and county health departments, local hospitals, and medical clinics have staff available for answering basic questions. For example, some hospitals have a program called Ask-A-Nurse, which can be a great way to get medical-related information. Getting the information you want may be as simple as consulting one of those pediatric charts that shows the average height and weight for children at each age. Many health-related Web sites also offer helpful information. The "Check It Out" at the end of this chapter (see page 24) lists a couple Web sites that offer reliable information on children's health. Of course, you can also make an appointment with your pediatrician.

On the other hand, if you're worried about your child's social, emotional, psychological, or intellectual development, it can be harder to find the information you need. Intellectual, emotional, psychological, and social development are far more difficult to measure than height and weight. There's more guesswork involved, and as a parent, your judgment on whether your child is normal often requires sorting through confusing and contradictory factors.

Here are five brief scenarios describing actual children. Even though they don't include information about the children's ages, read through the scenarios and try to imagine each child at whatever age comes to mind. Then, keeping in mind the age of the child you imagine, think about whether or not the behaviors described in each scenario seem normal or not.

Until about six months ago, Connor was generally a cooperative and cheerful child, but all that has changed. Now, "NO!" is Connor's first and favorite response to *everything* his parents ask him to do. Sometimes he adds, "I won't do it and you can't make me." If his parents force the issue, his protests get louder and louder. Sometimes he falls to the floor to resist his parents' requests.

Tobias's fears—especially at night—have been getting bigger and bigger. He's afraid to go to bed, talks of monsters lurking outside his window, and sometimes runs screaming into his parents' room in the middle of the night, agitated and panic-stricken. After shaking herself awake, his mother sometimes offers groggy reassurance. Other times, she provides rational explanations, and at still other times, she loses her temper, yells, and sends Tobias back to bed. She feels very sorry for Tobias and doesn't know how to help him.

Mika is constantly on the move. She gets into everything. She talks a great deal, blurts out comments when others are talking, and has a hard time sticking with anything she starts. She likes to bang things, yell, and make a lot of noise, no matter where she is. Over and over, her parents talk with her about her behavior, and she says she wants to do better, but then she quickly goes right back to being loud, wild, and overactive.

For several months, Tara has been incredibly moody. Not long ago, Tara was an even-tempered girl. Now she alternates between being very sad or very irritable, or sometimes, overly cheerful and silly. She also goes against whatever her parents ask her to do more than she used to; she avoids or objects to chores that she once did willingly.

Kenny has always seemed different—even "odd," but recently his differences have become worse. He doesn't look at others when they speak to him and he avoids eye contact most of the time. When his parents try to hug or touch him, he stiffens up and pulls away. Although he talks, mostly he repeats television commercials he's recently heard. He doesn't have normal conversations with friends or adults. His interests are very narrow; he spends much of his time playing with a broken radio.

As you can see from the preceding scenarios, children's behavior can be very different and very distinct. In real life, the parents in the scenarios were worried because their children's behavior didn't seem normal. What do you think? Are the behaviors described in these scenarios normal or not?

Your Child's Development: What's Normal?

After over a hundred years of human development research (and thousands of years of common sense), virtually everyone agrees that what's normal at one age may be abnormal at another. Of course, what's normal also depends greatly on your particular cultural and family setting. But generally, in the preceding scenarios, most of the children were displaying normal behaviors for their particular age group—behaviors that are expected, usual, and unlikely to signal a major problem.

For example, Connor's sudden defiance and other difficult behaviors are very typical of two- and three-year-old children. However, if Connor were age ten and still flopping down on the floor when he didn't want to do a chore, his actions would be out of the ordinary. Tobias's fearfulness is not unusual in three- to five-year-olds, especially if he's been exposed to lots of scary movies, video games, and storybooks. Tara's moodiness is relatively common for a child eleven to fifteen years old, but would be less so for a child six to ten years old. Similarly, Mika's talkativeness, loudness, and active behavior are normal among preschoolers, but her noisiness and rambunctious activity are unlikely to be considered normal (or tolerated) by the time she reaches mid-elementary school.

Throughout childhood and adolescence, every age has typical behaviors, some of which are endearing and some of which are puzzling or upsetting. Fortunately, most of these upsetting but normal behaviors fade away as your child matures.

Occasionally, certain behaviors are so odd that they wouldn't be normal at any age beyond the first months of life. For example, Kenny's behaviors—a strong aversion to touch, very narrow and repetitive interests, noncommunicative speech, and lack of social give-and-take—are very unusual and might represent a serious psychological disorder in a child at any age.

Your Child's Temperament

Parents with more than one child are often stunned at the differences between their offspring. They can't help but wonder how two children with the same family genes, raised in the same family environment, could possibly have such different dispositions. One may be outgoing and talkative, while the other prefers to play alone quietly. Or one might have a carefree spirit, while the other is filled with worries.

The huge difference that can exist between children in the same family is only a partially solved mystery. It's well-known that children are powerfully shaped by their family's values and behaviors, their neighborhood, the culture they live in, even the subtleties of their language. However, children are more than just a product of their surroundings. Children themselves also bring their own unique qualities into their families. In fact, some research suggests that this internal influence called *temperament*—a child's inborn tendency to behave in certain ways—can and does shape *parental* behavior (almost as much as parental actions shape the child's behavior). Think of a cuddly, happy baby who brings out smiles and hugs from her caregivers versus a colicky baby whose stiffness and aversion to touch can bring frowns, anxiety, and irritability to parents. Clearly, your child's temperament can affect you and your behavior. It's an interactive influence.

Some moms have told us how they knew, in advance, that their new baby would be a "wild child." If you've ever been pregnant, you probably already know how these moms knew about their baby's inborn behavioral tendencies even before the baby was born. The fact is, many children begin displaying their temperament *in utero.*

Two well-respected child development researchers, Stella Chess and Alexander Thomas, have identified nine different temperamental characteristics*. These characteristics are important not only because they're the seeds of your child's personality, but by learning to recognize them, you can better understand the distinct ways in which your child may be different from other children but still normal. Chess and Thomas's nine dimensions of temperament are listed on pages 13–14. Take a few minutes to consider your child's unique characteristics.

---

*Stella Chess and Alexander Thomas (1986). *Temperament in Clinical Practice.* New York: Guilford.

Nine Dimensions of Temperament

Activity Level

Children show a natural preferred level of activity that varies on the low end from slow and inactive to revved up and moving at the speed of light on the high end. This is the temperamental quality that pregnant moms often notice—because the unborn child is wiggling, squirming, and kicking long before she enters the world.

Tendencies to Prefer Things to Be Regular and Rhythmic

Some children prefer eating and resting in rigidly set patterns, while others have a lack of rhythm (even extending to sleep patterns—which most parents find rather disturbing). Even as adults, some of us prefer irregular sleep and meal times, while others like to eat every meal on a schedule and keep a regular bedtime.

Tendencies to Approach or Withdraw

Some children are open and interactive with animals and people around them—even when first meeting them. Others pull away, preferring to watch from a safe distance. Some even choose to withdraw entirely when possible. Children who are slower to get close to new people tend to be more cautious—they sometimes think long and hard before deciding to do something.

Adaptability to a Variety of Settings

Some children handle changes in what's going on around them easily. They sleep comfortably, play happily, and are fine with new surroundings. Others take much longer to become accustomed to changes. Some children simply seem to hate change and have great difficulty handling transitions. If your child has trouble with change, you'll especially notice it when she goes to and from day care, school, or another setting or activity.

Intensity of Response and Interactions

To some children, everything matters a great deal and they have strong and loud responses to even minor events. It's never hard to guess how these children feel about things. Others are more calm and less intense. These calmer children may just get quiet when they're upset and you won't even know they're feeling disturbed.

Responsiveness to Things Around Them

Some children have an inner or internal focus; they don't look around, listen, or pay much attention to what's going on around them. Others seem to take in a great deal of what is going on around them, and are responsive to what they see. The extremely responsive child may do best with just a little excitement, because if too much is going on she feels overwhelmed.

General Quality of Mood

Is the glass half full? Half empty? Some children are born with an inclination to be much more cheerful than others. Others are naturally more sad, negative, and pessimistic. Children who are hopeful and optimistic often are confident they can accomplish whatever they want to do.

Attention Span or Distractibility

Some children, even at an early age, will take something apart and then try, for a long time, to put it back together. They have a long attention span and a great ability to concentrate. Children with great concentration may also have trouble letting go of what they want to do and therefore resist mightily when their parent says "No." Other children can let go more easily, partly because they get interested in other things going on and forget about why they were upset or what they were interested in, in the first place.

Mode of Interacting with Others

Some children prefer to be the boss and in control, while others would rather follow the leader. Some children seek out reassurance and approval from people around them, while others are more independent, or even oblivious to the wishes of those around them. You can see these differences when you watch your child play with other children. Does she lead or follow—or do neither?

The "Nine Dimensions of Temperament" list underlines the fact that your child, like every child, comes into the world as a unique individual. Of course, your child's particular temperament doesn't excuse socially unacceptable behavior. As a parent, you naturally want to help your child have healthy relationships and live a productive life within the constraints of her own unique temperament. By having greater awareness of your child's temperamental tendencies, you can more easily anticipate problems and support your child in ways that encourage more emotionally, socially, and psychologically adjusted behavior.

To help you discover more about your child's temperament, here are some suggestions:

- Look back through the list of different temperamental dimensions and think about your child. Notice her particular tendencies in each of them.

- Keep her tendencies in mind as you read on and explore your child's unique quirks and potential problems.

- Study what the experts say about children's temperaments (see "Check It Out" on page 24 for a list of sources).

- Look for additional information on temperament throughout this book.

Determining What's Normal

In most cases, you're the best expert on what's normal behavior for your child. We say this because, since you've chosen to read this book, you're probably the kind of parent who has your finger on the pulse of your child's life and behavior. Because you live with her and care so much about her well-being, you're most likely very sensitive to your child's emotional ups and downs, to her social rejections and successes, and to her hopes and dreams. You're likely aware of everything, from her sleep patterns to her fluctuations in weight, eating patterns, and self-image. You're quick to notice and help her with everyday problems. But you're also probably the first to recognize when something seems disturbingly out of the ordinary for her, or for a child her age. This chapter will give you even more clues than you already have about how to determine when these behaviors are just normal quirks or signs of a potentially serious problem.

Partnering with a Professional

Because you're so familiar with your child, you're the one most likely to seek out an outside expert opinion when a problem arises that deeply concerns you. You may decide to get some professional guidance even when the problem isn't happening all the time. If it's bothering you a lot, an expert's reassurance that everything's normal or a diagnosis that pinpoints the problem exactly can help you do what's best for your child. In Chapter 11, you'll learn more about the various types of professionals in children's development and mental health, such as physicians, psychologists, counselors, and social workers, and how to choose the best one for you and your child.

If you do seek help, think of the professional as your partner. Each of you brings important information to the process. You bring loads of at-home information that the professional partner, quite simply, cannot know. She brings broad experience with children who have problems and an extensive knowledge base from which to make judgments and draw conclusions. She also brings training and experience in distinguishing between a diagnosable psychiatric condition such as attention deficit hyperactivity disorder (ADHD) and a more minor problem such as a highly active temperament.

An accurate diagnosis for your child is very important. In general terms, *diagnosis* is a label that helps professionals know what interventions might help your child's symptoms or problems. Just as a stomachache can signal anything from too much pizza to the presence of a bleeding ulcer, troubling behaviors in children can signal a variety of different disorders. A diagnosis should only be made after a very careful examination of your child, her symptoms, and her family, school, and neighborhood situation. If your child seems to need help beyond what you can give, then it's best to take her to someone trained to provide the help she needs. Parents, teachers, or other interested parties can offer valuable input, but only a mental health professional has the expertise necessary to make a meaningful diagnosis. We'll discuss more about what a psychiatric or mental health diagnosis is a little later in this chapter.

Some Helpful Questions That Give Clues to What's Normal

As we've noted earlier, knowing your child's age, developmental maturity, and temperament is important in figuring out what's normal and what's not so normal for your particular child. However, in addition, there are other guidelines to help you know whether your child needs professional help. Together with a mental health professional, you can explore a number of questions that can give you some helpful clues:

- Does your child say or do things that get in the way of doing ordinary daily activities?
- Do you or your child feel very upset about her behavior?
- Does your child act in ways that are especially unusual or odd?
- Is your child's behavior out of the ordinary compared to most children of her age, gender, and cultural group?
- Are there good reasons for your child's unusual behavior?

These questions represent some of the basic standards—the indicators or measuring sticks—that professionals will use to determine if your child's troubles require professional intervention. None of these indicators stand alone, but taken together, they can mean your child might need professional assistance. Let's take a closer look at each one.

Does your child say or do things that get in the way of doing ordinary daily activities?

Every child has problems at some time or another. For example, your child may get into a fight at school, suddenly start screaming and swearing at you, bite another student at day care, or be terrified of going to the dentist. But just because your child has a problem doesn't necessarily mean she's abnormal. And it certainly doesn't automatically signal a need for professional help. But if she's having considerable trouble doing her everyday activities, then she might have a problem serious enough for a psychiatric diagnosis. For example, if her fighting or biting is causing her to be suspended from school or banned from day care, then professional help may be needed.

As you can see, the bottom line for a professional to diagnose a *disorder* in a child is not whether a problem or symptom exists, but whether one or more of the symptoms is linked to a difficulty with everyday functioning—a *dysfunction*. Here are two common examples:

- If your child's emotions are mostly sad, and she has other depression symptoms such as problems sleeping, weight loss or gain, and a loss of interest in fun activities, *and* if these symptoms interfere with her school attendance or studies, then she might receive a diagnosis of *clinical depression*. (See Chapter 5 for more information on common symptoms of childhood depression.)

- If your child is very active, easily distracted at times, and rather impulsive, she may be diagnosed with attention deficit hyperactivity disorder (ADHD), but only if these sometimes normal traits interfere with your child's ability to function at school and at home. (See Chapter 4 for more information on ADHD.)

Also, it's important to know that displaying *one symptom* of a psychological problem doesn't mean that someone has a full-blown disorder. For example, a child might become sad about failing a test. However, unless this sadness continues and is accompanied by other depression symptoms that, in turn, get in the way of your child's regular daily activities, the sadness would not be considered a sign of clinical depression.

Do you or your child feel very upset about her behavior?

If your child is having a personal problem that keeps on happening, her problem might cause anxiety, guilt, anger, sadness, or fear in her—and in you or in other people who care about your child. If she's very afraid about being separated from you, she'll probably become agitated, tearful, and panic-stricken when such separations occur. Usually there's no doubt about it, your child is in great distress. And you're likely to be miserable as well.

On the other hand, an angry youngster who's being very defiant may be perfectly happy with herself, because using her defiant actions are getting her what she wants. However, her parents and everyone affected by her defiance may be in considerable distress.

Many *normal* problems are also distressing, and distress alone does not mean there is a true abnormal psychological problem. However, if the emotional or behavioral problems frequently cause someone—either parent or child—lots of distress, then a formal diagnosis may be in order, and treatment may be necessary.

Does your child act in ways that are highly unusual or odd?

Some behaviors are unusual and potentially troubling in children of any age. Here are examples:

- a child who has absolutely no social connection with anyone around her
- a child who frequently sees or hears things that no one else

sees or hears, especially if such experiences frighten or trouble the child and continue over time

- a child who has extremely unusual ways of thinking and communicating—again, especially if such thinking seems distressing and odd to the child and her parents

- a child who engages in repetitive behaviors over and over again for no apparent reason.

If your child engages in odd behaviors such as these, especially over an extended period of time, professional consultation is advised because she may have a diagnosable mental disorder and need treatment.

Is your child's behavior out of the ordinary compared to most children of her age, gender, and cultural group?

This question, commonly considered by professionals who evaluate children, is all about context. In other words, is your child's behavior normal or extreme for her particular context or situation? Consider the following scenario.

Your twelve-year-old son often rides a motorcycle without a license. He carries a knife with him, and sometimes a gun. He also has been known, on occasion, to kill animals. Does your child have a problem that warrants a diagnosis?

The correct answer to this question is: It depends on the social and cultural norms in his living situation. This is because if your son lives on a ranch in Montana, his behavior is probably normal because he's been raised in a context and culture that supports it. On the other hand, if you have a son and he lives in an urban area—say downtown Detroit, then his behavior may be a major problem, requiring professional evaluation and treatment.

Your child's behavior is always partly shaped by cultural input and circumstances. Because youth-oriented television and music lyrics often play up sexuality, profanity, and aggression, it can be hard for you to sort out whether your child's troubling behaviors are unusual for his age, gender, and situation. One interesting research finding is that children exposed to violent television are more likely to behave violently, whether they live in an isolated village in the Northwest Territories, in the Central American country of Belize, or in Los Angeles.

Professionals who evaluate children must consider cultural factors when deciding whether your child's way of behaving is normal or not. Certain behaviors would raise concern in one religious or ethnic group but not in another. For example, in some tribal cultures, people who have recently lost a loved one report hearing spirits of the departed calling to them as they go on to the afterlife. For mourners in these cultures, this experience is a normal part of grief. In contrast, there are other cultures where "hearing the departed calling" would be considered odd or abnormal, or even a sign of a diagnosable mental disorder.

Similarly, even though the same basic emotional problem may occur in several societies, it can be expressed differently from one culture to another. For example, in some cultures, depressed people report more physical symptoms such as headaches, fatigue, and bodily complaints than directly expressed feelings of sadness and guilt.

If you have a cultural background different from the professional helper who is trying to understand your child's problems, an extra effort on your part may be needed. Explaining your cultural or family norms to the professional, who may be unfamiliar with them, will help to assure that your child's diagnosis and treatment are appropriate for her. Again, this points to the vital role parents play in the partnership with a helping professional.

Are there good reasons for your child's unusual behavior?

Even when your child's reactions are unusually intense, you can often tell what triggered the reactions. She may have fierce and unreasonable temper tantrums, but only when she doesn't get what she wants. There may even be times when you can tell that something you've done has helped to set her off. However, sometimes childhood behavioral or emotional difficulties occur for no obvious reason. For example, your child may seem chronically sad though there has been no distressing event in her life to explain her sadness. Or she may be irritable all the time for no apparent reason. In extreme cases, your child's moods may alternate from very irritable to very sad to very happy, and it's not obvious why this is so. Generally, if there's no good explanation for your child's emotional or behavioral problems, then consulting a professional may help you figure out what's going on inside her to cause such disturbing behavior.

In summary, the preceding questions are basic guidelines that help us all—parents and professionals—determine whether certain troubles or behaviors signal that it's time for a child to get professional help. Of course, it's not necessary for your child to meet all the conditions represented by the preceding questions before you decide to seek help. Even one very troubling behavior may mean your child is in need of assistance.

And of course, just because a behavior is considered *normal* doesn't necessarily mean the behavior is good. As writer and psychiatrist Bruno Bettelheim wrote in his book *A Good Enough Parent*:

To be told that our child's behavior is "normal" offers little solace when our feelings are badly hurt, or when we worry that his actions are harmful at the moment or may be injurious to his future. It does not help me as a parent nor lessen my worries when my child drives carelessly, even dangerously, if I am told that this is "normal" behavior for children of his age. I'd much prefer him to deviate from the norm and be a cautious driver! *

Classifying and Diagnosing Your Child's Problems

Mental health professionals classify symptoms into groups to make diagnoses. This involves identifying specific problem behaviors and emotional experiences that usually occur together and attaching labels to these groups of symptoms. Unfortunately, this labeling process offends many parents and teachers, and could even make them hesitant to seek help.

Parents may say, "I'm not going to see a psychologist because all he'll do is label my kid and then she'll have to live with a label the rest of her life."

Labeling is, of course, a big part of how we communicate. If we didn't label similar items, we would be hopelessly bogged down in describing every detail. For instance, suppose we didn't have categorical labels for the common objects of everyday life and had to describe each of them physically every time we talked about them. If, instead of using the word *table*, suppose we had to say "that rectangular object with four legs and a flat surface made of wood" every time we wanted to refer to it. Communication would be nearly impossible. Likewise, labeling behavior patterns allows mental health professionals to talk about a child's difficulty in clearer, more consistent ways. And if we're all using labels in a similar way, it's more efficient than describing each individual behavior.

---

*Bruno Bettelheim (1988). *A Good Enough Parent: A Book on Child-Rearing*. New York: Vintage Books.

It's important to realize that though we may not want our children labeled by mental health professionals, they're going to be labeled by others—teachers, peers, coaches—regardless of our desire to have our children exist label-free. In fact, the behaviors and emotional states that lead a mental health professional to diagnose your child as clinically depressed might lead others to label her as inattentive, irritable, or dull. When children are experiencing trouble, and acting out or becoming withdrawn, it's likely some kind of labeling will occur, one way or another. It's better to have accurate labels that point to possible solutions, rather than labels that are judgmental and carry with them little hope for change.

Labeling unusual emotional and behavioral patterns also assists professionals in deciding how best to help. Different behavioral or emotional difficulties often require different forms of treatment. A child whose behavior fits a diagnosis of attention deficit hyperactivity disorder might profit from a behavior modification plan, special accommodations in school, and in some cases, medication. On the other hand, a child whose difficulties are better captured under the label "posttraumatic stress disorder" would usually not get a medication prescription. Rather, this child's treatment might involve play and talk therapy as well as learning relaxation skills.

When mental health professionals make a diagnosis, most of them rely on a book called *Diagnostic and Statistical Manual of Mental Disorders,* fourth edition, text revision (DSM-IV-TR) published by the American Psychiatric Association. This book, available to the public as well as mental health professionals, identifies patterns of emotional and behavioral difficulties in adults and children, and attaches labels (or diagnoses) to these patterns.

The DSM-IV is a very useful book, but it's only a guide; making an accurate diagnosis also depends a great deal on the training and subjective judgments of the professional using it. The disorders described in the DSM-IV often have symptoms overlapping with other disorders, making an accurate diagnosis difficult. This makes sense, in that troubling emotions and behaviors may be quite similar even when the causes of the distress are very different. People cry for many reasons. Children become irritable, anxious, or sad for many reasons. The DSM-IV makes an effort to group these troubling behaviors and emotions in meaningful ways, but doing so is a daunting task. Overall, the DSM-IV is far from perfect and certainly not the final word on understanding human psychological problems.

Indeed, the fact that it's now in its fourth edition shows how much ideas about mental health difficulties keep changing, evolving, and developing over time.

Despite its lack of perfection, many people in the mental health field find the DSM-IV useful in helping identify problematic patterns of behavioral and emotional difficulties and thereby, in planning effective interventions and treatments. In later chapters, behavioral and emotional characteristics based on the DSM-IV will be included so you'll have a sense of how these patterns relate to actual diagnoses.

More Things You Can Do to Help Your Child

If parents can't be expected (or allowed) to diagnose, what can they do? One parent told us she was beginning to think the main job of parenting was sitting around worrying. Yet, as you know, you are the central decision maker in your child's life, and your child's well-being depends on your active involvement in her life. As we've emphasized previously, for example, when it comes to determining whether or not your child has a diagnosable problem that needs treatment, it's crucial for you to take an active role and partner with whatever professional you've chosen.

In addition to getting an accurate diagnosis, an important piece of the partnership is this: Because you're the consumer—you're paying for the services—you're in charge of the process. Sometimes, because parents feel intimidated by professionals and all their academic knowledge and diagnostic labels, they forget this basic fact. So, keep in mind that because you're purchasing professional services, you deserve respect and a professional-parent partnership. Be assertive in providing information about your child, and ask your child's physician, psychologist, counselor, or social worker any questions you consider important. If you don't feel good about the services you're receiving, you can choose a different professional. If you live in a rural community, that may be hard, but when it comes to your child, getting a second opinion or driving to the next town to work with a different professional is well worth it.

Beyond being an active and involved parent, it's also crucial for you to educate yourself. Parenting is an art and a science. It requires commitment, education, support, practice, and this mysterious thing we call love. None of us can be expected to know everything about how to raise healthy, happy children on our own. Reading, parent education classes, and talking with other parents are just a few of the ways you can learn more about what's normal and what's not, and also learn how to help your child live a healthy, happy, and successful life. In each chapter of this book, a "Helpful Hints" section will offer you ideas and tips that you can use to empower yourself and your children.

Check It Out

DSM-IV Made Easy by James Morrison (New York: Guilford Press, 1995). If you really want to dive in and try to understand the Diagnostic and Statistical Manual of Mental Disorders, Dr. Morrison's book is a good starting place.

The Magic Years by Selma Fraiberg (New York: Charles Scribner's Sons, 1959). With humor and great empathy, Dr. Fraiberg brings you inside the infant's, toddler's, and preschooler's worlds. For its time, this is an amazing, sensitive, and insightful book that many parents and professionals still find helpful.

Making Us Crazy by Herb Kutchins and Stuart Kirk (New York: Free Press, 1997). Try reading this for an alternative and possibly radical perspective on the DSM system.

www.cdc.gov/growthcharts. The latest child physical growth charts, which were revised in May 2000, are provided here by the Centers for Disease Control.

www.childdevelopmentinfo.com. This Web site has excellent information on children's social, emotional, and intellectual development.

Here are three books that can give you a deeper look at temperament and how your child's unique, built-in, biological/physiological self predisposes her to certain personality styles:

Personality Plus for Parents: Understanding What Makes Your Child Tick by Florence Littauer (Chicago: Fleming H. Revell, 2000).

Temperament Tools: Working with Your Child's Inborn Traits by Helen Neville and Diane Clark Johnson, illustrated by Dave Garbot (Seattle: Parenting Press, 1998).

Understanding Your Child's Temperament by William B. Carey with Martha M. Jablow (Hoboken, NJ: John Wiley & Sons, 1998).

Chapter 2

Things That Go BUMP in the Night: Fears and Worries

> One of the other dogs was called Boon.
> He turned and said, "Your brother is in the chicken coop, and he won't come out."
> Howie ran and pushed his way past the other dogs. Then he looked through the little doorway. "Willy," he said, "you're not a chicken. You're a dog. Come out of there."
> Willy burrowed deeper into the nest of straw. Only his eyes and black nose showed. "It's too dangerous outside," he said.
> —Laurence Yep, *The Curse of the Squirrel*

In the opening quote from Laurence Yep's horror story for children, Howie is embarrassed for his brother Willy, because Willy is very scared and hiding in a pile of straw. This scene captures the central theme of this chapter—fear.

Although fear is a universal emotion, sometimes children and adults feel ashamed about feeling afraid. This might be partly because many cultures glamorize courage, bravery, and toughness. This attitude adds to the shame people feel about being afraid. For children, fear can be so undesirable that they feel afraid of being *seen* as afraid. Of course, Willy and Howie's story show that fear and anxiety aren't pleasant emotions, either for the person experiencing them, or for anyone nearby.

As a parent, you can easily become impatient and angry when your child displays seemingly irrational fears (after perhaps looking under your child's bed "for monsters" for the fifth time in a single night—at 3 A.M.). You may also feel embarrassed when your child acts terrified in public. Knowing how to help a child feel less fear or anxiety, and how to sort out your own responses, can be confusing.

Consider the following examples:

It's Monday morning, bright and early. Things at the Carson home are in turmoil. Eight-year-old Stacey is refusing to eat. She's crying, complaining that her head hurts, and begging to stay home rather than go to school. The night before, at bedtime, Stacey cried and told her parents she was afraid to go to school. She said the work was too hard, her teacher didn't like her, and other children stared at her. It was a familiar set of fears. In fact, more often than not, Stacey became upset when away from her parents for even brief periods of time. She was even trying to sleep with them at night.

+↓ ⫶ ⊁ ⊹ ⊹ 🇣 ⫶ 🇦 🇼 🇲

Ten-year-old John worries so much that his father calls him "Wally, the Worrywart." John worries about doing well in school and is often convinced his teachers don't like him. During soccer games, when not performing as well as he'd hoped, John tightens up and becomes so anxious he sometimes has to be removed from the game. He worries about events far in the future, such as taking standardized school tests that aren't scheduled for several months. He's often restless, tired, and irritable, and has difficulty concentrating.

+↓ ⫶ ⊁ ⊹ ⊹ 🇣 ⫶ 🇦 🇼 🇲

At the very thought of going to the doctor for a shot, eleven-year-old Mariah panics. She cries, throws tantrums, and even offers to do extra chores in an effort to keep from going. Upon arrival at the doctor's office, she attaches herself to her mother and acts like a terrified three-year-old. Mariah's powerful fear of shots emerged in third grade, shortly after a girl at school told her about fainting when receiving one.

+↓ ⫶ ⊁ ⊹ ⊹ 🇣 ⫶ 🇦 🇼 🇲

Stacey, John, and Mariah are all feeling fear associated with specific events and circumstances in their lives. Most of the time, your child's bouts with fear or anxiety are normal and pass without much difficulty. And often, fear has a protective function. Think about it: If your child had no fear, he might march right up to strangers and ask for money, start fights with boys much older and larger than himself, or decide to jump off the roof of your home. If he didn't feel apprehension about dangerous events, he might not avoid them or be energized enough to manage them successfully.

In young children, anxiety and fearfulness can be intense, as there is much about the adult world that doesn't make sense and can seem threatening. Sometimes, your child just needs some adult support or a little lenience while overcoming fears. However, other times, the support of parents and teachers isn't enough and professional help may be needed. The information in this chapter will help you decide whether you should simply comfort and support your child yourself or whether you should get some additional professional assistance.

What Are Fear and Anxiety?

Anxiety is an emotional state that includes feelings of nervousness, tension, and worry. Even though the words are sometimes used interchangeably, fear and anxiety are different. Fear is an immediate alarm response to a current situation that appears dangerous or threatening, such as seeing a grizzly bear ahead of you on the trail. Fear is present-oriented. Anxiety tends to be more future-oriented and involves worrying about lack of control over possible upcoming situations that seem threatening, such as earthquakes or burglars breaking into your house. Of course, this isn't a perfect distinction, and often, the terms are used interchangeably because they're so closely related, both in meaning and in personal experience.

If you've been fearful or anxious a time or two yourself, you know from experience that physical reactions and irrational thoughts often accompany these emotions. Typical physical reactions to fear include increased heart rate, nausea, upset stomach, blurred vision, headaches, and difficulty breathing. Mental reactions include unpleasant thoughts such as intrusive images of yourself or others being seriously hurt, looking foolish in front of others, making embarrassing mistakes, and so on. If your child is feeling fear or anxiety, he may avoid threatening situations, cry, bite his nails, tremble, fidget, suck his thumb, scream, look for a protector, or become absolutely frozen, unable to move. It's very painful for your child to experience any of these effects of fear—and certainly painful for you, as the parent, to watch and often feel powerless to help.

Considering Your Child's Age and Temperament

As noted already, being afraid and anxious is common in childhood. Between 10 and 30 percent of parents report having an overly nervous, fearful, or anxious child. Deciding what fears are normal, or at least what will pass with time and understanding, can be difficult. Certain fears are associated with specific ages or developmental stages of a child.

Common Childhood Fears

When the fear usually starts	What the child fears	When the fear typically resolves
Toddler/preschool Ages 2–6	The dark, strangers, dogs, thunder, other loud noises, ghosts, and monsters	Most of these fears resolve by age 8 or 9, but fears of the supernatural or movie characters tend to persist a bit longer
Elementary years Ages 5–10	Supernatural fears (ghosts, Dracula, Frankenstein, movie characters), bodily injury, and staying home alone	Mostly by age 12 or 13, but exposure to specific events can prolong these fears
Middle school Ages 10+	School performance (especially tests), physical appearance, accidents and death, and social rejection	Mostly by age 14 or 15, but nagging social fears and anxiety over physical appearance and school performance may continue

Of course, there are also common fears that emerge during adulthood. However, since this is a book about children, we'll let you generate your own adult list of fears—which may, of course, include having a fearful child! Suffice it to say, every stage of human life has accompanying common fears.

The tendency to be anxious or nervous varies greatly among humans. We all know people who startle easily or who, with little effort or preparation, have the ability to list every possible thing that might go wrong with the safest, most mundane plans. We also know people who are too busy hang gliding and rock climbing to notice just how scary the world can be. Not surprisingly, most of us are somewhere in the middle of this continuum of fearfulness, but the continuum extends naturally quite a ways in both directions.

Recently, we watched with interest as two sisters, ages nine and ten, encountered a waterslide. The younger of the two raced to the top and repeatedly and happily threw herself down the slide with reckless abandon. In contrast, her older sister, despite coaxing from their mother, occasionally looked up toward the big slide with visible discomfort, choosing instead to play quietly in waist-deep water. The mother wisely encouraged, but did not force, her more cautious child to engage in an activity that was clearly beyond her range of comfort.

The example illustrates how temperament plays a large role in each child's fear or anxiety. As noted in Chapter 1, newborn infants show basic temperamental differences on a number of different dimensions. One of these dimensions is the willingness to explore and adapt to new situations. If your child avoids new situations and has trouble adapting to them, he is more likely to struggle with anxiety. So, as described earlier, two children with very similar backgrounds, skills, abilities, and life experiences can experience life with remarkably different levels of anxiety. It's a basic, temperamental difference.

However, temperament is just a part of the picture. Life experiences, too, help determine anxiety and fear responses. Sometimes, exposure to a relatively normal situation can come at just the wrong developmental moment.

One of the authors of this book remembers, at age six, watching a movie about aliens abducting people and being profoundly frightened by it, though it didn't affect her younger siblings or older cousins much at all. For months, she refused to walk anywhere alone, and for a long, long time after seeing the movie, she had visions of everyone being stolen by aliens.

Other forms of learning play a role in the development of fear and anxiety. People can come to fear something simply because it's been paired with a pleasant or painful event.

One father told us about taking his toddler son to a high school basketball game for the first time. The gym was small and the cheering very loud. Each time the crowd cheered, his son would startle and cry. The father had to take his child home before halftime. The next time he took his son into the gym, the little boy started crying and refused to leave his father's side (actually his father's leg, to be more precise). It took a couple of years of maturation and of viewing basketball games on television in the family home before this little boy began relaxing in the gym.

Even though a child can learn to be afraid of a situation that is not normally frightening because the situation is paired with a painful experience, that fear does not have to be permanent. If provided with time and repeated pleasant experiences linked to the scary situation, the child can overcome his fear.

Sometimes, tragically, your child may be witness to, or involved in, traumatic events such as criminal attacks, violence, abuse, accidents, and natural disasters. Exposure to traumatic events is almost guaranteed to cause leftover anxiety symptoms (as we'll discuss further in Chapter 7).

Types of Anxiety

Problems with fear and anxiety show up in many forms. Some young children get very upset about being apart from their parents, while others are especially afraid of animals or very specific situations (like heights or talking in front of a group of other children). Learning more about the types of fear and anxiety in this chapter will help you decide whether your child needs professional help. You will also discover ways to help your child cope with both mild and more severe fear and anxiety.

Anxiety About Separations

Many young children are fearful when separated from their parents or other primary caregivers. This fear of separation is quite normal for young children—and sometimes for older ones. But about four percent of children have a serious *separation anxiety disorder*. These children feel extreme distress every time they're separated from their mom, dad, or other important caretaker, or from their home. Parents of these children describe the overarching symptom of separation anxiety disorder as "wild-eyed terror" at the prospect of such a separation.

Because all children experience separation anxiety from time to time, figuring out whether your child has the diagnosable form of separation anxiety can be tricky. A good starting place is to notice your own reactions to his behavior, such as:

- The thought of dropping your child off at day care (or leaving your child somewhere) seems dreadful and nearly overwhelming.

- For a month or more, it's been a big struggle for you to deal with your child's clingy, panicky behavior.

- You're feeling very concerned about your child's separation-related emotional meltdowns, which have been going on for over a month without relief.

If your own responses cause you to suspect that your child might have a separation anxiety disorder, next look through the following list of signs and note whether your child fits any of the descriptions listed. This checklist and the others like it used throughout this book are adapted from the American Psychiatric Association's *Diagnostic and Statistical Manual of Mental Disorders* (also known as DSM—see page 22 in Chapter 1). Because professionals use a similar checklist, it will be especially helpful for you to be familiar with what they'll want to know if you meet with them.

Signs of a Serious Problem with Separation Anxiety

❏ My child often experiences serious distress and protests mightily when I leave her at school, day care, or other places. This strong and repeated distress also sometimes happen when my child just thinks about being apart from me.

❏ My child often has big worries about losing one or both parents or about some harm coming to his parents or other people he feels close to.

❏ My child often has big worries about getting lost, being kid-napped, or other sudden events that might cause separation.

❏ My child often doesn't want to go to school—or refuses to go to school or other places away from home because of separation fear.

❏ My child often has bigger worries than most children his age about being alone, being without parents at home, or being without other important adults in other settings.

❏ My child often has nightmares about being separated from parents or other close adults.

❏ My child often won't go to sleep without being near parents or other close relatives. He is sometimes afraid of sleeping away from home.

❏   My child often has headaches, stomachaches, nausea, vomiting, or other physically distressing symptoms when separation occurs or is anticipated.

The separation anxiety checklist asks you to make subjective judgments that may be puzzling. For example, how can you tell if your child's behavior is considered "often" or if your child has "bigger worries than most children"? As a general guideline, observe your child over a one-month period; if you notice three or more of the listed behaviors described on most days during that time, your child may have separation anxiety disorder.

Getting Professional Help

Obviously, if your child has signs of separation anxiety disorder, you have an important decision to make. Should you take him to see a professional about the separation anxiety problem? Consider the following questions, and if you answer yes to one or more of them, it's probably time to consult a child development specialist or a mental health professional.

- Is the problem getting a lot worse even though you've been trying to help your child with it?
- Is your child, or are family members, in severe distress over the problem?
- Is the problem causing your child to miss out on normal and healthy childhood activities?

Once you decide to seek professional help for your child's separation anxiety problems, all you may need initially is a telephone consultation. Describe to the professional what's been happening with your child, and then ask for guidance. If you decide instead to meet in person for an initial consultation, there's probably no need to bring your child along. Doing so may cause unneeded distress.

After your initial consultation, counseling from a qualified professional may be recommended for you and your child. Fortunately, counseling has a strong track record of success with separation anxiety. Although the specific approach used will vary depending upon your child's age, the severity of his problem, and many other factors, overall, counseling will help you with new ideas, positive support, and guidance for coping with this challenging problem. It will also help you and your child realize he's not alone in experiencing such fears; many children go through the same thing, and help for their struggles is available.

More Ways You Can Help Your Child

Whether or not you seek the help of a professional, there are a number of things you can do at home that might bring some relief to you and your child. Look at the "Effective Approaches" list below. Note that, along with each of the six approaches, is a sample statement that demonstrates how you can speak to your child when using that approach. You may want to read through this list a few times and then come up with your own personal statements tailored to your situation.

Effective Approaches for Parents with Anxious and Fearful Children

Soothing Empathy: "It's a rotten feeling to be so scared.

Gentle Curiosity: "You seem scared. Want to talk about it?"

Comforting Reassurance: "Lots of people get afraid of things. I remember being really afraid of dogs."

Positive Encouragement: "I know it's hard to be brave about it, but I know you can do it."

Reasonable Limit-Setting: "Even though you're scared of spiders, you still have to go to bed."

Enormous Patience: "Yes, I'll help you walk by Mr. Johnson's dog again. I think you're getting better at it, though."

By using these positive approaches, rather than reacting harshly or impatiently, you can help your child's tension subside. Even though you may feel like telling your child to "buck up" and deal with his fear, forceful or negative messages invalidate your child's very real fears, and may only add to them. If instead you show empathy, encouragement, and even curiosity (but not too much attention), your child will be more likely to grow and mature beyond his fears.

Of course, along with these caring approaches, you may need to help your child successfully face the feared circumstances a few times, because if there's anything true about fear, it's the fact that it rarely disappears quickly or miraculously. Also, because children with separation anxiety have, to some extent, problems calming or soothing themselves, try some of the "Helpful Hints" listed below.

Helpful Hints for Your Child's Separation Anxiety

➤ Teach your child techniques for self-calming or self-soothing. Techniques might include:

- *Teach deep breathing through slow and careful bubble-blowing.*

- *Use soothing music on a regular basis to help your child learn to relax.*

- *Give him a transitional object or toy, such as a blanket, stuffed animal or worry-stone to hold or cuddle when you're away (and have him associate that object with comfort and relaxation).*

➤ Help your child learn and understand that 1) separations are a reality, 2) they can be fun, 3) they are temporary, and 4) reunions can be a fun ending to the time away:

- *With younger children, play peek-a-boo and "hide" for increasingly longer time periods.*

- *Make the real separations short at first, and build up to longer ones.*

- *Make a plan for separation by telling your child something like, "We'll get to day care, then I'll give you a big hug, and then I'll give you your fuzzy blanket to cuddle with. After that, I'll leave for work and you'll cuddle with your blanket and have fun till I get back." Be sure to tell your child you know he can handle it, but listen to his fears with compassion.*

- *Make sure the time you're away is filled with fun and is spent with kind people, doing pleasant things.*
- *Use humor as appropriate, such as "Yeah, but if I never went away, I couldn't ever surprise you with a present!"*
- *Reward your child for successful separations.*

➤ Check yourself and make sure that you're not doing anything that might be making the separations worse or contributing to the problem:

- *Don't let your own nervousness about leaving show.*
- *Avoid lingering too long or slipping away when your child is looking the other way.*
- *Never ridicule or dismiss your child's fears.*
- *Don't take away his comforting objects or strategies. Often parents get impatient with their children for dragging around a blanket or for thumb-sucking—both of which provide soothing and comfort.*

Specific Fears and Phobias

Some children experience intense fears about specific objects, animals, or situations. These unusual fears out of proportion to the threat are often referred to as *phobias*. For example, many children—and adults—are frightened of mice, even though a mouse presents a very tiny threat to a human.

A child can develop a phobia about most any object, animal, or situation. For example, some common phobias include intense fears of shopping, storms, blood, injury, elevators, dogs, birds, airplanes, loud noises, and social situations. And of course, some children (and adults) even have irrational, but strong, fears of clowns!

As with separation anxiety disorder, the main feature of a phobia is an almost paralyzing terror. The big difference is that in the case of a phobia, your child is extremely fearful of some specific object, animal, or situation (other than separation). These fears or phobias may result in avoidance ("Don't make me climb the ladder to the slide. . . . I don't want to!") or in strong efforts to escape ("Mommy, I want to get away from that doggy. . . . Now mommy, *now!*"). Some children fear social situations and try to avoid going places where they might be expected to interact socially.

Signs of a Serious Problem with a Specific Fear

❑ My child often has big and unreasonable fear touched off by the presence or anticipation of a specific object, animal, or situation (for example, fear of a dog or of riding in an elevator).

❑ When my child is exposed to whatever he fears, he almost always cries, has tantrums, freezes, clings to me or someone safe, and talks about being intensely afraid.

❑ My child is often intensely afraid of social or performance situations that include the presence of unfamiliar people or an evaluation by others.

❑ My child deals with strongly feared situations by avoiding them or enduring them with intense anxiety or distress.

If your child has any of the extreme fearful reactions described in the above specific fear checklist, and these reactions persist more or less steadily for over six months, your child may have a phobia-related problem.

Many people experience phobias but choose never to seek treatment for their fear. They live happy lives, avoiding rather than confronting, the fear. For example, if your child is deathly afraid of snakes, but you live in an apartment complex in the heart of a city, it's unlikely this fear will get in the way of anything but the viewing of occasional television nature shows. However, if you move to a rural setting where snakes (even harmless ones) abound, treatment may become more of a pressing issue.

Getting Professional Help

Here are two key questions to consider in determining whether or not your child should receive treatment for a phobia:

• Does your child's fear significantly interfere with his ability to participate in normal, healthy activities?

• Does your child feel overly upset by the fear, making him very unhappy or uncomfortable much of the time?

If your answer to one or both of these questions is yes, then it may be time to seek professional help. As with most fears and anxieties, counseling—as provided by any number of mental health professionals—is the most appropriate form of treatment for your child. Counseling for a specific phobia is usually straightforward and is often quite successful. The mental health professional may also encourage you to use some of the activities in the helpful hints for specific fears section on page 38 with your child.

One particular phobia that concerns parents and teachers alike is *school phobia,* also commonly referred to as *school refusal.* Many professionals classify school phobia as a form of separation anxiety, and although it was mentioned in the previous section, it deserves revisiting here. School phobia is by far the most common of all childhood phobias, and it is often quite distressing to the child and his family.

If your child is experiencing a school phobia, most likely your school will become involved because of repeated absenteeism, truancy, or complaints of nausea or other physical problems during school. If there are supportive teachers, counselors, and administrators at your child's school, a school phobia might be dealt with effectively through the school. On the other hand, because of the many other demands on school personnel, it's not unusual for schools to be ill-equipped to handle your child's problem. Often, it's necessary for parents to enlist the aid of an outside mental health professional to assist in getting the child back into school as quickly as possible. Most experts agree that children with school phobia should get right back into school before staying home becomes an entrenched pattern.

In addition to seeking professional help, try to find out if there are any specific events at the school, such as bullying, that are causing or contributing to your child's fears. Also, take note of any ways you as a parent may be inadvertently contributing to your child's difficulties with school. There are several ways this might be happening:

- Your child may be picking up on *your* worries about him.
- If you have lots of fun with your child when he stays home, he could be staying home because he's getting so much positive attention from you.
- Your child might think he has to stay home to take care of you or someone else at home.

Helpful Hints for Your Child's Specific Fears

➤ Modeling is a powerful learning tool. Don't show off, but demonstrate your own "nonfear" of the thing or activity your child fears. Even better, when doing so, talk to yourself in a positive and constructive way: "I'm holding this snake and I feel fine. I'm doing great. It feels so good to be able to handle this snake and not be frightened."

➤ Offer to do the feared activity with your child a number of times, and then gradually fade yourself out.

➤ Have your child learn to relax his body and mind and talk to himself in a positive and soothing way (teach him to say, "I'm doing fine," "I'll be okay," "I can feel my muscles relaxing," and other confidence-building self-talk statements).

➤ Remember to be encouraging rather than shaming. Listen rather than argue. Let your child feel scared and experience exposure to the scary thing at a distance. This is especially helpful if it happens to include your child witnessing other children having fun with the feared event or item.

➤ Try exposing your child to the feared thing in small doses or parts, or try "successive approximations." For instance, if your child is showing some fear of dogs, try getting some stuffed animal dogs. Then try visiting very small puppies at a pet store. Then try a little larger puppy, and so on.

➤ Give your child coping strategies. One parent we worked with had a child who was afraid to go into the bathroom. He was afraid something might jump out of the toilet. This child's mom taught her son a happy song to sing when going into the bathroom. At first she went into the bathroom with him, singing the song. Then, she began to wait outside while he went in. They would both be singing. Eventually the boy overcame the fear and was able to venture into the bathroom independently, without singing.

➤ Ask your child to rate his fear on a scale of 1–100, with 100 being "scared to death" and one being completely calm. By using a measurement system, both you and your child can begin understanding what sort of things are frightening and what sort of coping strategies are more or less helpful.

Generalized Anxiety

Some children have a *generalized anxiety disorder.* In contrast to what we've been talking about—separation anxiety and specific fears and phobias, generalized anxiety disorder is broader in nature, encompassing a variety of fears and worries. Some people describe generalized anxiety disorder as the fear of everything, as children or adults with this condition seem to almost look for something to be afraid of in virtually any situation. A good example of someone with generalized anxiety disorder is the storybook character Chicken Little, who repeatedly expressed anxiety over his belief that "the sky is falling!"

If your child has generalized anxiety disorder, you will notice two main features:

- He worries about a wide range of problems, dangers, and possibilities beyond his control.
- He feels like he can't control his worrying.

This double-whammy of worry becomes a sort of personality style for the child. He carries the style with him almost constantly, anticipating serious negative consequences way before they could happen. He rarely or never feels relaxed or peaceful. As you can see, this type of anxiety can be a constant burden for a child—not to mention his parent! This is one reason why, if your child has generalized anxiety, he may also often be tired; when children carry the burden of anxiety around all the time, it takes up lots of their energy.

Signs of a Serious Problem with Generalized Anxiety

❑ My child feels restless, keyed up, or always on the lookout for something bad to happen.

❑ My child is easily and often tired.

❑ My child has trouble concentrating or complains of his mind "going blank."

❑ My child seems more irritable or jumpy or reactive than most children.

❑ My child complains of, or obviously has, extra muscle tension.

❑ My child has consistent trouble with falling asleep, staying asleep, or having restless, unsatisfying sleep.

If your child fits at least one of the descriptions on the general anxiety checklist on page 39, and he's in significant distress or his anxiety gets in the way of his normal daily activities, then it's a good idea to get professional help.

Getting Professional Help

In most cases, the best approach for dealing with generalized anxiety is, once again, some form of professional counseling. Usually counseling focuses on helping children develop skills for coping with nervousness and anxiety.

For example, one child we worked with had a fabulously active imagination. This little girl could think of wildly complex things that just might go wrong, and she could do so in almost any life situation. "What if we go to lunch with Grandma, and the elevator is broke, so we have to take the stairs and she has a heart attack?" "What if I don't have the water hot enough when I wash the dishes, and some germs stay on there? But what if I get it too hot and it burns me?" Her parents, after years of trying to reason through her fears, had grown quite weary and impatient with her. One strategy we introduced was to have her write her fears into short stories with frightening details and gory scenes. The only rule was that to get her reward (a combination of extra allowance and going out to lunch), the story had to come out all right in the end. Move over, Stephen King!

Helpful Hints for Your Child's Generalized Anxiety

➤ Try using massage techniques, including back rubs or foot rubs, or rubbing other body areas where your child carries tension. Research shows that regular massage has a positive effect on a wide range of emotional and physical problems.

➤ Teach your child to practice deep breathing, listen to soft music, and use other meditation strategies for focusing and reducing stress. (This is a great idea for anxious kids *and* for parents made uptight by their anxious kids!)

➤ Set aside a specific time to allow your child to talk about what he finds frightening. Listen carefully, but don't argue. When the time is up, thank him for sharing his fears and anxieties, and reassure him that you will do your best to make sure his life is as safe as possible. Also reassure him you can talk again at the

next appointed time about these fears and worries, but that
you don't really want to talk about the fears in between times.
Of course, if an emergency happens, you should still talk with
your child immediately. But if he brings up a minor worry at a
time other than your designated worry-talk time, then you
might say, "Hey, that's a great thing for us to talk about during
our worry-talk time."

➤ Help your child begin to understand the power of our brains.
Talk about how we can make ourselves feel very frightened, or
very sad, or even very happy, just by thinking about certain
things. Have him remember a funny story you both know. Tell
it, and laugh about what happened. Then, have him talk about a
frightening time, and notice how doing so made him begin to
feel afraid. Learning to control emotions by refocusing thinking
is a lifelong challenge, but anxious children can feel more hopeful and more in charge of their feelings if they begin to learn
how to do this.

➤ Reward your child for his occasional bravery in the face of life's
difficulties. You might try stickers, stars, surprise rewards, or,
occasionally, a shared food treat like ice cream. (Be very careful
about regularly using food as a reward for your child. You don't
want him to get hung up on food as an emotional reward;
doing so can lead to obesity or other eating-related problems.)

Other Anxiety Disorders

There are also other forms of anxiety-based problems. In particular,
many children have obsessive-compulsive disorder and posttraumatic stress disorder, which are discussed elsewhere in this book
(for a brief mention of obsessive-compulsive disorder, see Chapter
10; for posttraumatic stress disorder, see Chapter 7).

What About Medication for Children with Anxiety Problems?

There are no medications that actually cure anxiety, but certain
prescription medicines have a calming effect. Interestingly, the
medications usually prescribed to help anxious children fall into the
category of antidepressants. These drugs have not been evaluated for

their long-term effects on children. For these reasons, mental health professionals generally don't consider medical treatment to be a desirable option for children who are experiencing anxiety. In extreme or severe cases, physicians may prescribe medications, but these are to be used with caution. At best, prescription drugs offer a short-term aid to calm children while they learn new coping skills. If your child has debilitating anxiety that's not responding to home remedies, school interventions, or mental health counseling alone, a consultation with a medical doctor such as a child psychiatrist might be helpful. The doctor may prescribe medicine as a temporary measure to help your child work more productively in counseling and interact more easily in other settings.

Summing It Up

Fears and anxieties are natural parts of the human experience. There are times when it's both healthy and wise to be anxious or afraid. There are also times when it's important to overcome our fears and become involved in life despite them. Children face many challenges in learning to handle their fears and sometimes things get hung up in that process. A frightened or anxious child cannot sleep well, play well, or learn well. You can do many things to help your child become less fearful and anxious. But when patience, love, safety measures, good modeling, and the passage of time don't help, then it's time for professional assistance.

Check It Out

A Light in the Attic by Shel Silverstein (New York: HarperCollins Children's Books, 1981). Poems by Shel Silverstein often have themes of fear or anxiety expressed in warm, silly ways that can facilitate discussion with a fearful child. We especially recommend the poem "Whatif." It's a great example of a child suffering from generalized anxiety disorder.

Cool Cats, Calm Kids: Relaxation and Stress Management for Young People by Mary L. Williams (Atascadero, CA: Impact Publishers, 1996). This is a great book if you're looking for creative strategies for teaching your child how to relax.

Helping Your Anxious Child by Ronald Rapee, Susan Spence, Vanessa Cobham, and Ann Wignall (Oakland, CA: New Harbinger, 2000). Here is a great step-by-step guide to help parents deal with an anxious child.

I Don't Know Why . . . I Guess I'm Shy: A Story About Taming Imaginary Fears by Barbara Cain (Washington, DC: Magination Press, 1999). This storybook helps younger children (ages 4–8) better understand the nervousness or shyness they feel when around other children.

Perfectionism: What's Bad About Being Too Good? by Miriam Adderholdt and Jan Goldberg (Minneapolis: Free Spirit Publishing, 1999). If your child's anxieties stem from worries about not being perfect, this book is the practically perfect choice.

Stress Can Really Get on Your Nerves! by Trevor Romain and Elizabeth Verdick (Minneapolis: Free Spirit Publishing, 2000). This book is an easy read aimed at children ages 8–13 who need help understanding and managing their stress. It's factual, humorous, and very reassuring.

There's a Nightmare in My Closet by Mercer Mayer (New York: Dial Books for Young Readers, 1974). This is our favorite book to recommend for anxious children. It provides a nice and understandable model for dealing with fear.

Where the Sidewalk Ends by Shel Silverstein (New York: HarperCollins Children's Books, 1974). This is another excellent book by this author. The poem "Sick" provides a humorous look at life from the perspective of a child with school phobia.

Chapter 3

Troubles with Bodies: Sleeping, Eating, and Toileting

> He didn't want to sit down anyway because of the soft, uncomfortable load in his pants, which had been there all afternoon and which felt cold and squishy when he moved too much.
> **—Sharon M. Draper, *Forged by Fire***

Though we may not want to admit it, most of us have a love-hate relationship with our bodies—their looks, limits, troubles, and break-abilities. All around us, on view 24 hours a day, are artificially created "ideal" youthful bodies, making it harder than ever to accept personal imperfections and limits. It's even hard to accept natural differences that are neither imperfections nor limits. And to make matters worse, our bodies sometimes betray us. Bones break. Backs give out. We get exhausted, yet can't fall asleep. There's really no end to the problems our bodies give us.

Children have their own special challenges with their bodies. They often scrape a knee or cut a finger. They accidentally wet their pants, or like the little boy in the chapter's opening quote, soil them. They may have frequent tummy aches or earaches, or suffer from allergies. Having a child with physical difficulties, including troubles with weight, peeing or pooping, or sleeping, can be one of the most frustrating and scary experiences you can have as a parent. These last three problems, in particular, feel so *out of your control.* This chapter is designed to reduce your fears and frustrations by focusing in on what might be wrong in those cases and what you can do about it.

Beyond the everyday irritations and worries related to their bodies, some children feel ashamed of their bodies or body functions. These feelings of shame often begin in childhood because of messages from peers, parents, teachers, and the media. Children are especially vulnerable because they often get teased by their peers, and even by adults, about their size, looks, and even their color. Parents, teachers, and other caring adults have a daunting task to help children learn to be accepting of their bodies and live comfortably in them.

Consider the following troubles:

When Haroun was five years old, his mom began finding soiled underwear in his drawers and under his bed. When she asked him about this, at first, he said the underwear wasn't his. He blamed his younger brother, and sometimes claimed that neighborhood friends were leaving their underwear at his house. His mom didn't challenge his stories, but simply told him to be careful.

However, the rather smelly problem kept reappearing. After several confrontations, Haroun admitted that he had "done number two" in his pants, and said it was because he was too busy sometimes to go to the bathroom, but he would try not to do it anymore. However, rather than getting better, the problem continued to worsen.

Eventually, through tears, Haroun told his mom that he wasn't always sure when he had to go anymore, and told her that sometimes, when he took off his clothes, he found poop in his pants, but he didn't even remember pooping. By this point, Haroun's mom was becoming very frustrated with him and tried punishing him with a removal of TV whenever she discovered poopy underwear. Unfortunately, the consequences didn't seem to help with the pooping problem, and Haroun became withdrawn, angry, and defensive.

Eight-year-old Elizabeth had never gone more than two weeks in her life without wetting the bed. Her parents had tried rewards, nagging, ignoring it, and active punishment, all to no avail. Just when everyone got their hopes up that the problem was over, it started all over again. It was beginning to affect Elizabeth's social life, because she feared spending the night away from home or having people spend the night with her, worried that an episode would happen and she would be teased and humiliated. Elizabeth seemed to genuinely want to bring the problem under control and even tried not drinking anything after dinner in hopes that she wouldn't wet the bed. Her parents were somewhat comforted by the fact that both of Elizabeth's older brothers had had similar difficulties, but they had outgrown them at an earlier age.

Jonathan had always been something of a night owl. Even as a very young child, he had a very difficult time settling down at night, and now at age ten, this pattern continued even though he had to get up early in the morning to go to school. Jonathan would lie awake at night for long periods of time before finally falling asleep. As a result, he was tired and sleepy during the day and on several occasions during school had fallen asleep in class. A couple of times a week, he took naps after school and tended to sleep for long periods on weekends.

Jonathan's parents tried all sorts of ways to help him fall asleep, including back rubs and soft music. They also tried being very forceful with him and demanding that he shut his eyes and go to sleep. His parents were convinced that his tendencies to be irritable in the afternoon were related to the lack of sleep, but were increasingly at a loss as to how to help him with this.

Sarah's parents noticed with some alarm that she'd begun refusing to eat healthy meals. In addition, she was eating far less than usual and had begun talking about having "fat legs." Even at eleven, Sarah and her friends were aware that thin is a cool and popular way to look, while fat is ugly, shameful, and unpopular.

Sarah's mom was especially worried because she had struggled with an eating disorder in high school. As Sarah began losing weight, her parents began trying to force her to eat. The ensuing "food wars" got very intense, making mealtime miserable for everyone.

These stories might seem rather disturbing and hopeless. Of course, our point here is not to upset or discourage you, but to point out how children's bodies and minds are intimately connected. The thoughts they think and the emotions they feel affect their physical health. For example, they can make themselves physically sick by worrying, complete with headache, stomachache, and reduced immune function. On the other hand, their physical condition also affects the way they think and feel. A bad head cold or the flu can leave them depressed and irritable and emotionally drained, feeling unable to cope with ordinary stress. You may recognize the same body-mind connection from your own experience.

Virtually any physical problem can have psychological dimensions, and virtually any psychological problem can have physical dimensions. In this chapter we won't cover every possible disturbance your child may have, but we'll focus on three all-too-common problems directly related to the body-mind connection—difficulties with elimination patterns, sleep, and body image.

Troubles with Toileting

In children especially, a basic function like toileting can have emotional and psychological meaning. For example, if your child soils or wets herself or her bed, she may do so in part because of stress or as a part of a brewing conflict between the two of you; you want the child to pee and poop into a toilet, while she is quietly opposing or angrily defying your wishes. At other times, the reasons for the peeing and pooping problems may be unclear, and in some cases the problems may have purely physical origins. Obviously, your child's psychological state and social relationships are affected by these difficulties with peeing and pooping, regardless of what's causing the problem.

The stories earlier involving Haroun and Elizabeth illustrate common childhood problems with the natural process of eliminating body wastes. *Encopresis* is the official name given to the tendency to poop into inappropriate places such as into clothing, on the floor, in the bed—even into the houseplants! It is the diagnosis a professional would probably give your child if the child meets all these criteria:

- is at least four years old
- poops into an inappropriate place at least once a month
- does so for three consecutive months

Enuresis refers to urinating in inappropriate places, either at night, during the day, or both. Enuresis is the diagnosis you could expect if your child meets all these criteria:

- is at least five years old
- pees in inappropriate places at least twice weekly
- does so for three consecutive months
- *or* if it happens less often, it causes personal distress or interferes with normal activities

While the physical inconveniences of these problems are considerable, the social stigma is probably worse. Social events such as overnights and camps may be dreaded or impossible if your child has elimination problems, and bring on shameful feelings for her. If you or other family members blame her for these problems or take her "accidents" too personally, your social embarrassment and anger can contribute unnecessarily to additional shameful feelings. In particular, punishing or yelling at your child, acting embarrassed, or trying to make your child feel ashamed tend to make the problem much worse than it would be otherwise.

Therefore, professional help may be called for, and can make a big difference in your child's overall development and self-esteem. Not only can professional help begin solving the problems, it can also help you and your child feel more normal about the situation and cope in more positive, accepting ways.

Considering Your Child's Age and Temperament

Hardly any parents truly enjoy changing diapers, discovering soiled sheets, or watching their child embarrass herself by losing bladder control in a public place. Consequently, many parents feel great relief when their child can wear big-boy or big-girl underwear.

Unfortunately, the hassles of diapers and the impatience of our culture often cause parents to have unrealistic expectations regarding their child's toilet learning, which can lead to parental frustration and anger. We want to emphasize that there's nothing officially abnormal about boys and girls wetting their beds until at least age five and there's nothing abnormal about children pooping their pants until at least age four. Even further, many experts believe that some children, especially boys, are often not neurologically equipped to control their bladders and bowels—even by the ages listed above.

If your child is a late-bloomer with regard to potty training, you might seek parent education or support in this area, or even consult a professional. But the truth is, toddlers develop at different rates, and sometimes have different priorities or agendas than their parents in this very personal developmental job. We know from our experience as parents that it's easy to think our children should accomplish these developmental milestones much sooner than is realistic. Again, our point is that it's important to relax your expectations and realize that what's normal is often very different for different children.

Your child's temperament may also come into play. If she has a free-spirited, independent, exploring personality, she is going to take less happily to the hassle of going to the bathroom. If she is more oriented toward pleasing others and gaining social approval, she will likely potty train more easily. Potty training can become quite a power struggle with certain personalities, and we highly recommend that you do some reading and reflection on how to keep from getting all tied up in such a struggle (be sure to look over the resources on pages 62–63). Of course, personality alone is only a small part of the picture, and certainly not the whole explanation for trouble with elimination.

Diagnostic Considerations

If your child is having problems with pooping after turning four, or with peeing after turning five, or those problems have come back after she has mastered bowel and bladder control, it's time for a visit to your physician. Problems with soiling or wetting can be due to such general medical conditions and related causes as:

- chronic diarrhea or diabetes
- side effects from some medications
- severe constipation (as it becomes increasingly painful for your child to poop, she may hold in the feces, but eventually "leakage" occurs and soiling results)
- urinary tract infection
- problems with the muscles that should keep the urine in the bladder
- a family history of enuresis (about 75 percent of all children with enuresis have a close relative who has also had the problem)

If the physician examines your child and concludes there's no physical or family history cause, then we suggest you talk with a mental health professional. Even if there *is* a physical cause, you might want to consider counseling as well. Learning to manage bowel and bladder problems is challenging for both children and their families. Elimination problems could also be due in part to a child's emotional distress or to a desire to show independence or opposition to the parent's wishes, and getting some guidance on how to deal with those causes as well can be very helpful.

Getting Professional Help

Your first stop in seeking professional help is the physician, as just discussed. But if you decide to seek treatment from a mental health professional, what should you expect? There are several fairly effective approaches for treating these problems. For encopresis, the usual treatment is *behavior modification*. The counselor will help you set up a system of rewards and other actions that you can use to get your child to change her pooping habits.

A behavior modification plan for encopresis may include:

- giving your child positive rewards for pooping in the toilet
- giving minimal attention to your child when she poops in other places
- requiring her in a nonpunitive way to help with the clean-up
- setting up a star chart or some other system for consistently rewarding positive behaviors

For enuresis, treatments include:

- behavior modification (as above)
- a bell-and-pad device
- clinical hypnosis
- medications

The *bell-and-pad device*, available at most drug stores, is a moisture sensor that you place under your child at bedtime. If your child starts to wet the bed, the sensor detects moisture, and a buzzer or bell sounds, awakening her. Your job is to coach your child to respond to the buzzer by getting up and going to the bathroom.

When *hypnosis* is used with enuresis, the counselor will help your child to imagine or visualize the mechanics of bladder control and release, and guide her to talk with her bladder. She might learn to say something like, "Okay bladder, I'm going to listen to you closely at night. So when you get all filled up I'll feel that and then I'll get up and go pee-pee in the toilet. And then I'll go back to bed and you'll be empty and I'll be nice and dry. Okay? So be sure and let me know when you're full. I'll be listening."

The point of this visualization and bladder talk is to help her understand the mechanics of a full bladder and urinating. It will also help her recognize that getting up and going to the bathroom in the night might be within her realm of control.

If *medication* is needed for enuresis, a low dose of antidepressant medication will probably be prescribed. Interestingly, the reason for the prescription will be for the drug's side effects. This medication has a general drying-out side effect that, although uncomfortable to many people who take it for other reasons, allows enuretic children to make it through the night without peeing in the bed. Sometimes the medication is used in conjunction with other procedures, usually the bell-and-pad device.

About 70 to 75 percent of children with enuresis respond successfully to each of the last three treatment approaches. If you use the bell-and-pad device with your child, you'll also need to use the behavior modification strategies described earlier for encopresis.

Unfortunately, not all children with encopresis and enuresis respond to treatment. If your child continues to struggle, you have several options:

- Obtain a more intensive medical examination.

- Help her develop what may be a lifelong strategy for coping with her problem, such as using a diaper at night.

- Continue to support and encourage her as you wait for her to grow out of the problem (which doesn't happen until age eight or ten for some children).

Things to Think About Concerning Common Treatments for Enuresis

Behavior Modification
- It's a good tool for shaping and teaching your child appropriate toileting behavior.
- It takes discipline and follow-through on your part.
- Some children won't cooperate because they're not interested in doing what you want them to do, and therefore they refuse to respond to rewards or consequences.

Medication
- It's quick, convenient, and effective.
- The problem often returns after stopping medication.
- You might feel reluctant to give your child medication.

Bell-and-Pad Device
- It's effective.
- It's somewhat of a hassle.

- Your child may dislike it.
- You might feel uncomfortable about strapping a device on her bed that will buzz or chime in the middle of the night.

Hypnosis
- It's effective.
- It might take longer than the other approaches.
- Your child feels more in control.
- You might be reluctant to have your child hypnotized.

There's a high likelihood that children will eventually outgrow enuresis and encopresis problems, even without professional intervention. It's rare for elimination problems to persist into late adolescence or adulthood. Encopresis that continues into late childhood or early adolescent years tends to be more difficult to clear up than enuresis.

Helpful Hints for Your Child's Bowel and Bladder Problems

➤ Have empathy for your child's situation. Hardly any children enjoy wetting the bed or pooping in their pants. It's crucial for you to clearly express empathy or sympathy for your child's problems by saying something like, "Oh honey, I'm so sorry you wet the bed again. That must feel pretty awful."

➤ Be sure to recognize that the problem is the child's, not yours. Also, just because your child has elimination problems doesn't mean you've failed as a parent. Unfortunately, as a parent, you're even less in control of your child's bladder and bowels than she is. A healthy response is to let your child experience her problem and her embarrassment and then give your support.

➤ Avoid using punishment, scolding, or ridicule as a response to bladder and bowel problems. These approaches will only increase your child's anxiety and shame, and may actually decrease her ability to control the problem.

➤ Read books with your child that are written to teach children about bowel and bladder control. Two of our favorites, *Everyone*

Poops and *Dry All Night,* are listed in the "Check It Out" section on pages 62–63.

➤ Use a team-oriented style of encouragement. This might involve saying things like, "I know we can do it," and then providing rewards for positive results and empathy. Or "That's too bad, but I bet you'll succeed next time," for negative results.

➤ Set up a concrete behavior modification reward system.

➤ Consider making dietary changes, such as eliminating caffeine or particular foods that your child may be sensitive to.

Troubles with Sleeping

Healthy sleep patterns are important for your child. If she sleeps poorly, she may:

• experience fatigue and low energy

• worry about going to bed, dreading the possibility of not being able to go to sleep, stay asleep, or sleep comfortably

• struggle with bad moods—be less tolerant, more easily frustrated, and more irritable

• appear sleepy and inattentive throughout the day

• become agitated and emotionally raw

• aggravate other conditions she may have, such as anxiety or attention deficit hyperactivity disorders

Sleep researchers have found that as many as one-third of children in kindergarten through fourth grade have at least one sleep-related problem. Very young children with sleep difficulties often end up in their parents' bed for a portion of the night; once this habit is established, it can be very difficult to break. When conflicts about where your child ought to be sleeping develop, it's stressful for both you and your child. In most Western societies, sleeping separately from parents is encouraged from birth onward. In some other cultures, however, sleeping in the family bed is considered normal; children sleep with their parents for years. Some Western parents believe in the *family bed* and are comfortable with joint sleeping arrangements. Parents who practice *attachment parenting,* which fosters emotional and physical closeness between parent and child, encourage children to stay as close to their parents as they want to, in order to insure emotional bonding. Depending upon your own personal preference and comfort, you may want to use the family bed or the attachment parenting philosophy in your home (see "Check It Out" on pages 62–63 for more information on these two approaches).

There can be many causes for sleep difficulties, such as illness, allergies, stress, physical discomfort, changes in environment, developmental changes in your child, changes in your family or home, anxieties, medication reactions, and so on. Consult a medical professional if your child has persistent problems with sleep. With severe and disruptive sleep problems, an evaluation by a neurologist in a sleep clinic may be the best course of action.

Considering Your Child's Age and Temperament

Sleep needs vary remarkably by age and by individual. Winston Churchill slept only five hours a night, supplementing his sleep needs with catnaps, but most people can't use this strategy without getting spacey and irritable.

On average, sleep needs decrease with age. Babies often sleep 14 to 18 hours a day (although they usually manage to be awake and crying when their parents are trying to sleep). Young children often need about 10 to 12 hours of sleep per night, along with daytime naps. Generally, teens need far more sleep than they get. Most researchers believe that the average teen needs 8 to 9 hours of sleep per night, but because of busy schedules and a general resistance to sleep, they get less than 8 hours (although many teens sleep into the afternoons on weekends—perhaps to catch up on sleep needs). The ability to fall asleep and stay asleep ranges widely across the population, and is influenced by genetics, biology/physiology, learning and habits, and trauma.

Problems with the Sleep Process

Children can have trouble with falling asleep, staying asleep, and experiencing sleep that is refreshing.

Signs of a Serious Problem with Sleeping

❏ My child has trouble going to sleep or staying asleep most nights. This has lasted for at least a month. She's usually very tired during the day and either feels very upset about her sleep problems or the problems interfere with her regular activities.

❏ My child has been sleeping way more than normal children her age for over one month.

❏ My child's sleep patterns seem way out of whack. She's awake when she should be asleep and sleepy when she should be awake. It's almost as if she's become nocturnal.

❏ My child is regularly overcome by an irresistible urge to go to sleep. These bouts of sleep occur quickly, are brief and refreshing, and have been happening for over three months.

The symptoms on the checklist above represent four major sleep problems, usually referred to as:

- insomnia (difficulty sleeping)
- hypersomnia (sleeping too much)
- circadian rhythm sleep disorder (sleep schedule is flipped around)
- narcolepsy (sudden intrusion of sleep into daily activities)

If your child is experiencing any of these problems, it's worth a visit to her physician. Depending upon the outcome of that visit, further observation and evaluation by a neurologist at a sleep clinic or lab may be warranted. Although medications are sometimes prescribed for sleep difficulties, question your child's physician closely about whether the medications are likely to disrupt your child's natural sleep cycles and whether the medications have addictive qualities or adverse side effects.

Other Problems Associated with Sleeping

Sleep problems that include odd behavior or unusual emotional and physical arousal during sleep are generally referred to as *parasomnias*. Take note of whether your child experiences any of the following unusual sleep-related behaviors.

Signs of Other Big Sleep Problems

❑ My child repeatedly awakens with detailed recall of extended and extremely frightening dreams. Her dreams often include threats to her survival, security, or self-esteem.

❑ My child often awakens abruptly from sleep, usually within the first couple hours after she's gone to sleep. The awakening often starts with a terrible scream, but when I try to comfort her, she doesn't seem awake and she doesn't recall the screaming or awakening the next day.

❑ My child often rises from bed during sleep and walks around, usually within the first couple of hours of sleep. During this time, she usually has a blank stare, is hard to awaken, and doesn't remember sleepwalking the next day.

Some of the problems listed on the other sleep problems list above are often more entertaining than distressing. For example, we've heard stories about children who, while walking or talking in their sleep, urinate in the bathtub or laundry hamper, or speak with great enthusiasm, while at the same time being completely incoherent.

On the other hand, even the most innocuous sleepwalkers can suddenly engage in unsafe activities. For example, we know of children who have walked barefoot out into the subzero Montana temperatures in winter and of children who have walked or climbed out of fourth story windows. Children's sleep disturbances can be very unsettling for parents.

By the time Melissa and Rolando scheduled a consultation appointment, these young parents were almost accustomed to their nightly ritual. It went something like this: After juggling their busy schedules during the day, and enjoying early evening family time, they were thrilled to put Maxie, their four-year-old daughter to bed. Occasionally she'd fuss a bit, emerge from her room, and crawl into her parents bed, but Melissa or Rolando would gently take her back to her own bed and she'd drop off to sleep. Then, about two hours after she was sound asleep, Melissa and Rolando were shocked back to reality by an intense, high-pitched scream from Maxie's room. They would bolt from bed and find Maxie in acute distress, writhing in her bed.

Sometimes her eyes were open, other times not. The scream always seemed to come out of nowhere and was followed by 15–20 minutes of howling and wailing. If they tried to pick her up and soothe her, Maxie just howled louder and stiffened her body. And the most puzzling part of the whole scenario was that, when the morning came, Maxie didn't remember any of it.

Sleep terrors may be more disturbing for you than for your child. The bad news is that they tend to persist off and on for years. The good news is that they probably won't have a lasting, adverse affect on your child. On page 58 are some tips on responding to sleep disorders, including sleep terrors.

With all sleep disorders, medical evaluations may be necessary to rule out physical causes. If, as is often the case with nightmares, night terrors, and sleepwalking, your child's problem is not medically related, be especially careful when choosing a mental health professional to visit. Look for someone with significant experience and training in this area.

Even if the sleep problems have some physical basis, a mental health professional can be an important part of the treatment for a number of reasons. First, sleep pattern changes and sleep deprivation can be signals or symptoms related to other disorders. It's important to screen for these other possibilities and treat the whole child, not just one symptom. Also, a knowledgeable counselor can help by assisting parents in analyzing the sleep problems and making a good plan for improvement.

More Ways You Can Help Your Child

Sleep is one of the few human activities that cannot be improved by trying to do it. We've all had the miserable experience of trying to fall asleep, and many of us have had the frustrating experience of trying to make a child fall asleep. It doesn't usually work. However, you can gently create conditions to help your child more easily fall asleep and stay asleep. Be careful to avoid creating conditions that end up causing other family disruption, such as allowing the child to sleep on the couch or—if it's an area of couple conflict—in the parents' bed.

Helpful Hints for Your Child's Sleep Problems

➤ For problems with the sleep process:

- *Develop a sleep schedule and routine for your child. For example, get on pajamas, have a snack, brush teeth, read a short story, crawl in bed and snuggle, say a little prayer, or reflect on a good thing about the day, and then lights out.*

- *Provide quick rewards for your child if she stays in bed and really tries to go to sleep.*

- *Make sure your household has a regular schedule for meals, recreation, and sleep.*

- *Make sure your child is getting enough exercise and fresh air.*

- *Have a nightlight or two, agree to leave the door open a crack, promise to check on the child in a half-hour (and don't forget to do so).*

➤ For other problems with sleep:

- *If your child wakes up from a nightmare, be very reassuring. Do not dismiss her fears. Let her crawl in bed with you and tell you about her bad dream and then gently return her to her own bed. (Unless you're practicing the family bed or attachment parenting philosophy, in which case your child would already be in your bed.)*

- *If your child has a night terror, try to provide comfort, but realize that she may not respond to you in a positive way. You can try telling stories, humming or singing a lullaby, or gently stroking your child while talking in a soothing voice. These procedures may not make much of a difference, but at least they give you something to do.*

- *If your child is prone to night terrors, try to adhere to a regular sleep schedule and minimize disruption from that schedule.*

- *If your child is a sleepwalker, do your best to keep her safe. Close observation is important. Remember, it's perfectly okay to wake her up and direct her back to bed.*

Troubles with Body Image and Eating

Eating patterns and preferences vary greatly in humans. Some children are hearty eaters, others very picky. Changes in eating patterns or sudden weight loss or weight gain can signal a number of possible problems, including depression or specific medical disorders (such as hyper- or hypothyroidism). However, one common problem, faced especially by girls in our culture, is that being thin has become a major standard for femininity. Even before adolescence, it's not uncommon to hear girls complain that they are "too fat." Many young girls also develop fears about their current and upcoming natural body changes.

With television, movies, magazines, and video games all beaming impossibly "perfect" bodies at children, it's no wonder that body image, self-esteem, and eating behavior are greater struggles for children of recent generations. Girls, of course, get the message that they simply can't be too thin, too graceful, or have skin that's too smooth and wrinkle-free. Boys get the message that masculinity is equated with being big, strong, and muscle-bound (and even with having a hairless chest!). Some children begin changing their eating or exercise patterns to try and achieve these impossible body types. This behavior can lead to metabolic changes, mood disturbances, and sleep, energy level, and nutritional imbalances. It also begins vicious dieting and weight-gain cycles that can plague children for the rest of their lives.

As a preadolescent, your child is unlikely to develop a diagnosable eating disorder, but it's useful for you to know the basics about eating disorders in case signs of it do show up. The most common of these disorders are anorexia and bulimia. A child with *anorexia* will eat extremely little food, lose weight or fail to gain weight normally, and be intensely afraid of becoming fat. A child with *bulimia* will also fear becoming fat and will sometimes eat a huge amount and then force herself to throw up. Overall, a child with bulimia doesn't lose much weight, but has major body image struggles.

Be on the alert for the following:

- tendencies to under- or overeat
- repeated statements about body dissatisfaction
- experimentation with throwing up after a meal
- unrealistic weight-related goals or expectations

School counselors or teachers can also be good observers and informants, and they sometimes organize effective individual or group interventions to help children who are struggling in this area. However, if your child changes eating habits in a significant way, loses weight, or seems overly concerned about body size, it might be wise to consult with a mental health professional who specializes in this area. Anorexia is difficult to treat and can severely affect both social and physical development. Eating disorders, in their most serious forms, are deadly.

Also, be on the alert about any ways you might unwittingly contribute to your child's body image struggles. Because of the media's emphasis on extreme thinness as attractive, it's tempting to urge "chubby" children to eat less, or to feel sorry for children who are less attractive by these narrow standards. Children are astute observers. They easily pick up on their parent's disappointments. We all need to work on widening our definitions of attractiveness, and to grow in our appreciation of diversity.

The Seriously Overweight Child

Today's sedentary lifestyles and ready access to vast quantities of fats and sugars are creating an alarming number of overweight children. Remember to stress healthy eating, exercise, rest, and balance with your child. If you're seriously concerned about your child's weight:

- Consult with your family physician or pediatrician.
- Learn together, as a family, the healthiest ways to eat and engage in physical activities.
- Consult with a mental health professional if your child needs more help with eating problems or losing weight.
- Look for groups, organizations, and other opportunities that might be of help. Your mental health counselor can suggest some resources.
- Accept your child as she is, and help her accept, take care of, and appreciate her body.

Helpful Hints for Your Child's Eating or Weight Problems

➤ Limit television time, and screen and comment on magazines, video games, posters, and other negative body-image influences

➤ Make absolutely sure your child gets physical exercise, even if she is both super-*un*athletic and quite unmotivated. Try table tennis, dog walking, fencing, dart throwing, bowling, hiking, or whatever other creative activities you can think of. Work with her until you find something she can do regularly.

➤ Limit snacking and especially soda intake.

➤ Encourage consumption of lots of veggies and fresh fruit.

➤ Dads, make sure your daughters know you admire them, and that you regard them as interesting for nonphysical reasons. Let them know you love them, appreciate them, and respect them from the inside out.

➤ Moms, teach your sons to respect their bodies, and the bodies of females.

➤ Genetic factors play a large role in your child's body size or shape. So, don't get overfocused on this issue because you'll only make your child feel bad about something she can't change much.

➤ Take care of yourselves. Model healthy living. Don't fuss and diet all the time. Eat well, exercise, and love the body nature gave you.

Summing It Up

Your child's mind and body are intimately and endlessly connected and interactive. Her thoughts and emotions will affect her physically and everything happening in her physical body will affect her mentally and emotionally. This is especially true if your child is having trouble with her bladder, bowels, sleeping, eating, or body size. When her mind-body problems take up more and more of the day, when they become the focus too often, and when it just doesn't seem like anything you've done is helping, then it's time to get professional help. Most of these challenging difficulties can be managed or completely eliminated if you follow the guidelines in this chapter or obtain professional help.

Check It Out

Baby and Toddler Sleep Program: How to Get Your Child to Sleep Through the Night, Every Night by John Pearce (New York: Perseus Publishing, 1999). Parents who want to set up good sleep habits will find this book helpful. Though primarily focused on younger children, many useful suggestions that will help with older children are included.

Dry All Night: The Picture Book Technique That Stops Bedwetting by Alison Mack (New York: Little, Brown & Company, 1990). If your child suffers from bedwetting and you'd like a gentle, nondemanding home-based approach to solving the problem, try this picture story that you can read to your child or she can read to herself.

Everyone Poops by Taro Gomi, translated by Amanda Mayer Stinchecum (LaJolla, CA: Kane/Miller, 1993). To the delight and disgust of its readers, this popular book contains 27 picture-pages of the backsides and poop of various animals and humans as well as unanswered questions like "What does a whale's poop look like?" The message is: We all eat and we all must poop. This book is not for squeamish parents.

Family Bed: An Age-Old Concept in Child Rearing by Tine Thevenin (Knoxville, TN: Avery Publishing, 1987). This book supports the attachment parenting model mentioned in this chapter by giving parents permission to have their children sleep with them in the family bed.

Killing Us Softly 3 by Jean Kilbourne, produced by Sut Jhally (Northampton, MA: Media Education Foundation, 2000). For an understanding of the pressures children face regarding body image and body size, this is a chilling video. Now in its third edition, the video explores the incredibly damaging messages we get about bodies from the advertising world. We don't recommend watching this video with your children until you've previewed it yourself. The content is condensed and the ads she uses are graphic. The benefit of watching is to understand the power of the messages your children are getting thrust at them, day and night. You can better empathize with their struggles (and your own).

No More Bedwetting: How to Help Your Child Stay Dry by Samuel J. Arnold (Hoboken, NJ: John Wiley & Sons, 1997). Written by a urologist, this book helps parents figure out how to handle different types of bedwetting, including anatomical, psychological, or sleep-related problems.

Raising Boys: Why Boys Are Different—and How to Help Them Become Happy and Well-Balanced Men by Steve Biddulph (Berkeley, CA: Ten Speed Press, 1998). The author considers the most important issues in boys' development from birth to manhood and explains the parenting and guidance boys need.

Real Boys: Rescuing Our Sons from the Myths of Boyhood by William S. Pollack (New York: Penguin, 1999). Pollack challenges conventional expectations about manhood and masculinity that encourage parents to treat boys as little men, raising them through a toughening process that drives their true emotions underground.

Reviving Ophelia by Mary Pipher (New York: Ballantine, 1994). This book explores the amazing drop in self-esteem and increased vulnerability experienced by girls when they begin adolescence.

The Right Moves: A Girl's Guide to Getting Fit and Feeling Good by Tina Schwager and Michele Schuerger (Minneapolis: Free Spirit Publishing, 1998). This book encourages girls to reach their full potential by developing a healthy self-image, eating right, and becoming physically fit.

Taking Charge of My Mind & Body: A Girls' Guide to Outsmarting Alcohol, Drug, Smoking, and Eating Problems by Gladys Folkers and Jeanne Engelmann (Minneapolis: Free Spirit Publishing, 1997). Using first-person stories, this book helps young women make responsible choices about how to treat their minds and bodies to stay healthy and strong.

There's a Nightmare in My Closet by Mercer Mayer (New York: Dial Books for Young Readers, 1974). This book is fun to read and can help with talking about dreams, nightmares, and sleep troubles.

www.attachmentparenting.org
This site offers information on *attachment parenting,* an approach to parenting that seeks to build a strong parent-child emotional bond by focusing on and responding to children's needs for physical/emotional closeness and touch.

Chapter 4

Problems with Attention, Hyperactivity, and Impulsivity

> It was one of the most exciting things, to get into another world than your own regular world, especially at a time when the regular world or things you had to do in it bored you.
> —**Mary O'Hara,** *My Friend Flicka*

Attention deficit hyperactivity disorder (ADHD) is one of the most well-known childhood behavioral difficulties. It affects an estimated three to five percent of all U.S. elementary school-age children. Many children in other countries also meet the ADHD criteria of being highly impulsive, inattentive, and overly active.

In an age as busy and full of distractions as ours, it's hard to know what a normal and healthy level of activity and attention span might be. And although ADHD has become a common diagnosis only in recent times, Ken, the main character in the old classic *My Friend Flicka,* written by Mary O'Hara in 1941, would easily qualify for this diagnosis. It's also known that Thomas Edison, John F. Kennedy, Amelia Earhart, and others of great influence acted in ways that might fit an ADHD diagnosis. So, it's clear that while the label is new, the troubles (and perhaps advantages) associated with this condition are not.

This chapter will help you sort out your child's normal youthful vigor from more problematic symptoms of ADHD. In addition, we'll focus on whether your child needs help and what kind of help is needed. To help you get a taste of how children with ADHD or ADHD-like symptoms behave, consider these two children:

Six-year-old Patrick was at it again. His mom said, "Stop running through the kitchen," but Patrick kept dashing back and forth by the stove as if he was dodging bullets. His dad told him, "Keep your hands to yourself and don't you touch your sister or you'll be in time out!" but Patrick was climbing up on his older sister's shoulders like she was a jungle gym.

In the midst of this evening family chaos, his mother looked through Patrick's book bag and found it crammed with papers, books, broken crayons, a half-eaten banana, and assorted pieces of trash. She also discovered a note from the teacher expressing concerns about Patrick's behavior at school. The note said that Patrick was making careless mistakes, had a difficult time sticking with anything, and often didn't follow through on what he was asked to do. This was the third teacher note Patrick's mother had received. After the first and second notes, she talked with him about his behavior, and both times, he sincerely expressed his desire to change. Unfortunately, Patrick's sincerity was clearly overshadowed by his hyperactivity and impulsivity.

+1 7 5+1+1 7 5+ +

By age nine, Shaundra was well-known as the classroom space cadet. More often than not, she needed three or four sets of instructions from her teacher before she "got it." Shaundra was a daydreamer. Many times, she'd start an assigned project and then wander away, leaving it half-finished. Other times, she rushed through assignments, paying little attention to detail. Her rush was usually motivated by her teacher, who had promised Shaundra a reward if she actually finished something.

At home, Shaundra's parents saw the same pattern. She left her bed half-made, the dishes partly done, and often forgot to feed her pet rabbit—even after they began grounding her for not finishing things. She resisted doing homework, and to insure that she would really finish her school assignments, she usually needed at least one parent sitting beside her the entire time. Shaundra's older brother and younger sister were both highly responsible straight-A students, and Shaundra's parents' tendency to compare Shaundra to them made it harder for her to measure up to the family standards.

+1 7 5+1+1 7 5+ +

Do you have a child like Patrick who's often overexuberant and acts before thinking? Or is your child like Shaundra, a daydreamer and easily distracted? The ways Patrick and Shaundra behave illustrate two different types of ADHD. In addition, although Patrick's actions seem to fit the description for ADHD, he may not necessarily be diagnosed with this condition—we'll discuss the different diagnostic criteria later.

If your child is acting like Patrick or Shaundra, you may already be thinking about taking him to see a doctor or mental health professional. These problems of inattention, hyperactivity, and impulsivity are incredibly frustrating, and they are among the most common reasons why parents like you bring their children to mental health professionals. But how can you know if your child is simply a normal, albeit excitable or spacey child, or a child who may be suffering from deeper problems, even diagnosable problems that require professional treatment?

What Is ADHD?

ADHD has three main *features:*

- inattentiveness or distractibility
- hyperactivity or overactivity
- impulsiveness or acting without thinking

Many examples of these behaviors are included in checklists later in this section.

In addition to having these three features, ADHD appears in three *forms or types.* Each of these types includes one or more of the main features. The three types are:

- predominately inattentive type
- predominately hyperactive/impulsive type
- combined (inattentive and hyperactive/impulsive type)

Does Your Child Have ADHD?

Look at the lists of signs or symptoms—one list for each of the first two types—on pages 67 and 68. These lists are based on the diagnostic criteria for ADHD published by the American Psychiatric Association. You can use them to help you determine if your child needs an evaluation for ADHD. If your child shows evidence of both of these types, he may receive the "combined" diagnosis. For each item on the lists, consider whether your child engages in the listed behavior not just once in a while, but often.

Signs of a Serious Problem with ADHD—Predominately Inattentive Type

❑ My child doesn't attend closely to details or often makes careless mistakes in schoolwork or other activities. My child's work is almost always messy, incomplete, or performed carelessly.

❑ My child has difficulty keeping his attention on tasks and play activities. He quickly moves from one uncompleted task to another.

❑ It doesn't seem as though my child listens when someone speaks to him. He seems tuned out, or not to hear things that have just been said.

❑ My child doesn't follow through on instructions and fails to finish things. He understands the instructions to do chores or homework, but his inattention keeps him from following through. He isn't being defiant, he's just not paying attention.

❑ My child can't seem to organize tasks and activities, and keeps basic materials in disarray.

❑ My child avoids or dislikes tasks that require continued mental effort, such as schoolwork or homework.

❑ My child frequently loses things necessary for tasks, such as school assignments, books, and pencils.

❑ My child is frequently distracted, moving from task to task, often leaving several tasks incomplete because his attention is drawn to the next opportunity.

❑ My child is forgetful in daily activities.

Consult a mental health professional about a possible diagnosis of the predominantly inattentive type of ADHD if:

- Your child shows at least five of these behaviors more commonly than most children of his age.
- These behaviors are interfering with basic areas of his life such as school and social relationships.

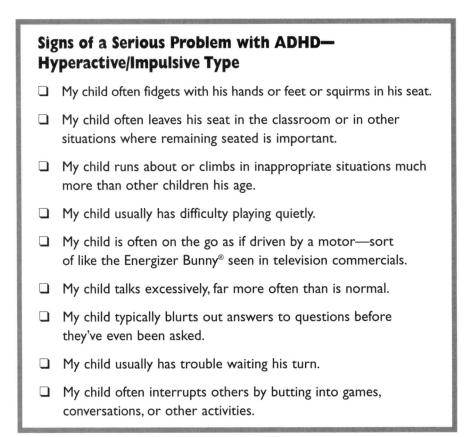

Signs of a Serious Problem with ADHD—Hyperactive/Impulsive Type

❑   My child often fidgets with his hands or feet or squirms in his seat.

❑   My child often leaves his seat in the classroom or in other situations where remaining seated is important.

❑   My child runs about or climbs in inappropriate situations much more than other children his age.

❑   My child usually has difficulty playing quietly.

❑   My child is often on the go as if driven by a motor—sort of like the Energizer Bunny® seen in television commercials.

❑   My child talks excessively, far more often than is normal.

❑   My child typically blurts out answers to questions before they've even been asked.

❑   My child usually has trouble waiting his turn.

❑   My child often interrupts others by butting into games, conversations, or other activities.

Consult a mental health professional about a possible diagnosis of the predominately hyperactive/impulsive type if your child displays at least five of the behaviors on this list to a significant degree over at least a six-month period. Mental health consultation can help determine if your child is suffering from ADHD.

Finally, if there are at least five characteristics present in both the inattentive and the hyperactive/impulsive areas, an evaluation can help determine if your child has combined type ADHD.

As with most behavior-based problems, more boys than girls suffer from ADHD symptoms. However, that's not to say that girls don't experience these difficulties. Sometimes, because of temperament, different socialization, or different expectations, girls might be less dramatically hyperactive and impulsive. Therefore, they may not be as quickly recognized as needing assistance with their problems. Also, it appears that girls often suffer from attention problems that go unnoticed.

Maybe It's Not ADHD

It's easy to look at the ADHD checklist criteria established by the American Psychiatric Association and conclude that your child, your friend's children, your friend, and even you have ADHD. We (the authors) come to these conclusions about ourselves all the time. During workshops we often put the ADHD diagnostic criteria up on a screen and lead everyone in the room in a rousing game of self-diagnosis. Of course, over half of the studious, conscientious, high-achieving people in our workshop audience discover they meet the diagnostic criteria for ADHD. And we once worked with a twelve-year-old girl who decided, on her own, that she should come for treatment because she read about ADHD in a *Newsweek* article.

This quickness to self-diagnose ADHD is because all of us sometimes experience inattentiveness, hyperactivity, and impulsivity. The symptoms exist along a continuum; no one has an attention span that lasts forever. In fact, most of us don't have attention spans that last as long as we'd like them to. Fortunately, within ADHD diagnostic criteria there are items that actually limit and clarify when the diagnosis is more likely to be accurate.

It's NOT ADHD When . . .

- Your child's symptoms and behaviors are annoying, but not interfering with his normal daily activities at home or at school.

- Your child seems terribly inattentive, hyperactive, and impulsive, but so do 99 percent of the other children of his age and gender.

- Your child only has serious troubles stemming from his inattentive, hyperactive, or impulsive symptoms in one setting. (For ADHD to be diagnosed, your child must have ADHD-related problems in at least two different settings, usually at home and at school.)

- Your child has never had symptoms that caused big troubles at school or home until sometime after age seven. (Because ADHD is a chronic condition that begins in early childhood, it cannot begin after a person has turned seven. If ADHD symptoms do emerge, then it's a sign of a different problem.)

- Your child has had his problems with ADHD symptoms for less than six months.

Considering Your Child's Age and Temperament

Because ADHD has become so commonly diagnosed and discussed, it's not unusual for parents of busy, curious children to be told by friends, relatives, or even strangers—at the airport or in the grocery store—that their child might have ADHD. The truth is, many children have energy levels that rival the child with ADHD. And children, at certain developmental levels, sprint their way from one activity or exploration to the next at a speed their caregivers find unnerving. As we've discussed, neither high energy levels nor distractibility are signals of ADHD by themselves. And both are variable, due to age, temperament, situation, and occasionally even sugar consumption.

Schools and teachers often have little patience with active, energetic, disruptive, distractible, and sometimes irresponsible children. Partly because of this impatience, ADHD has become the most well-known of all child behavior problems. Additionally, more is being done to help children who display many ADHD-like symptoms but don't meet the criteria for the diagnosis. In particular, many books have been written for parents who have children who look, act, and feel very much like children who have ADHD. Several resources in the "Check It Out" section on page 77 can acquaint you with alternative ways of looking at the sort of misbehavior commonly linked to ADHD.

What Causes ADHD?

ADHD is generally considered to be a brain-based disorder. In other words, the prevailing belief is that the parts of the brain that influence self-control and self-direction aren't functioning very well. There may be disturbances in brain chemistry, or there may be too much or too little activity in certain brain structures. However, despite this view that ADHD has biological and brain-based causes, so far no one has identified a specific biologically-related disease process or specific brain damage that directly causes ADHD symptoms (although children with brain damage from lead toxicity or fetal alcohol syndrome often show ADHD-like symptoms). Also, since the problem frequently runs in families, experts suspect that heredity plays a significant role, although this is certainly not the only reason a child might suffer from ADHD. A number of other possible causes have been suggested, such as diet and certain vitamin deficiencies, but no one knows for sure how much of a role they play in most ADHD cases.

One thing most experts agree on is this: If your child has ADHD symptoms, you're not completely and directly to blame. However, if you use inconsistent discipline, don't communicate well with your child, or have inadequate or inconsistent rules in your home, your child's ADHD symptoms may worsen. For example, regularly scolding your child for his natural biologically-based hyperactive behavior seldom helps ADHD-related problems. Also, if you're too negative with your hyperactive or inattentive child, it may damage his relationship with you as well as his self-esteem.

By contrast, there are ways you can reduce your child's ADHD symptoms. These include:

1. consistently giving positive feedback ("You're doing a nice job working quietly on your homework, Mario.")

2. communicating clearly and effectively ("When you're done with your homework, then you can call your friend and go out and play.")

3. providing immediate, but small negative consequences paired with encouragement for inappropriate behaviors ("Uh oh, Mario, you haven't finished your homework, so you can't go play tonight, but I bet you'll choose to work hard and go out and play tomorrow.")

These approaches can help your child learn the sort of behaviors that will help him succeed in school, at home, and in his social relationships. Additionally, if you have a child with ADHD symptoms, he'll need your positive attention, ongoing support, and active presence in his life to help him learn to control or decrease the behaviors that get him in trouble.

Getting Professional Help

If your child's behavior is extremely disruptive, it's very important to seek professional help. With all the self-help information available, you might believe you can make the diagnosis yourself, but a *professional* evaluation is crucial if you strongly suspect your child has ADHD. An accurate diagnosis of ADHD is important because:

- Some research suggests that certain medications may be particularly effective in helping with your child's neurological and physical-based symptoms (see the books by Silver and Barkley in "Check It Out" on page 77).

- Recent research indicates that the single most effective method to quickly suppress ADHD is to use stimulant medications such as Ritalin, Dexedrine, and Adderall.

- Only a careful evaluation by a professional can tell you whether using such medication is appropriate for your child. If your child's problems with inattention, hyperactivity, or impulsivity significantly interfere with his ability to get along with others, perform at school, or carry out home responsibilities, we encourage you to get an evaluation right away.

It's especially important to have an evaluation done as early as possible. The longer you and your child struggle with these symptoms, the more likely he is to develop other difficulties related to being hyperactive and inattentive. For example, if he gets a lot of negative feedback because of his symptoms, he may develop a bad attitude toward authority figures and become aggressive, or he might become anxious, depressed, and withdrawn.

Another important reason to seek a professional evaluation if you suspect your child has ADHD is that there are a number of other possible diagnoses that might be more accurate. Many childhood and even adult disorders have symptoms in common with ADHD. Children who are upset over their parents' divorce, depressed, anxious, or sleep-deprived may be overactive and inattentive. Getting an accurate diagnosis will help ensure that your child gets the right help for his condition or situation.

A professional evaluation is not the end of the story. Perhaps more than any other diagnosis, ADHD is a controversial and confusing condition. For example, some professionals do not even believe that ADHD exists (they think it's a product of our impatience with the natural disruptive behavior commonly associated with being a boy). In addition, other professionals are strongly opposed to treating ADHD symptoms with medications (see "Check It Out" for more information). With all this disagreement, even among professionals, what's a concerned parent to do?

Deciding whether to have your child take medications for an emotional or behavior problem can be one of the most difficult choices you can face as a parent. We wish we could tell you exactly what to do, but that's impossible, because every child and every family situation is different. Generally speaking, we recommend the following steps when considering medication:

- Try the "Helpful Hints for Your Child's ADHD" on pages 75–76.
- Try getting counseling for your child or for yourself or for your family.
- Educate yourself in a balanced way on the pros and cons of using medication for ADHD (see resources on both sides of the controversy listed in the "Check It Out" section).
- Make your decision about medication based on what you think is best for your child and your family.

As you may already know, there is no known cure for ADHD. Instead, it requires careful management. Medications and other interventions are aimed at helping alleviate symptoms and allowing your child to grow and develop successfully. You may find comfort and solid guidance by maintaining an ongoing consulting relationship with a professional as you raise a child with ADHD. It may also give you hope to know that about 30 percent of children diagnosed with ADHD will recover from the disorder by around age 15 or 16.

"But He's Not Always Like That"

You may find the fact that your child sometimes behaves perfectly to be especially frustrating and puzzling. At times your child may control his activity level and successfully direct his attention to a task, especially when he's highly interested in something, such as video games or television programs. This occasional burst of apparent self-control can make it seem as if these children are willfully engaging in problem behavior much of the time. To illustrate this tendency,

Mary Sheedy Kurcinka, in her book *Raising Your Spirited Child* (see page 77), quotes an old Ziggy cartoon that reads: "We are able to process your call. We just don't feel like it." However, as Kurcinka points out, and this is confirmed by research and common sense, your child's ADHD symptoms are almost always unintentional. The fact is that many hyperactive, inattentive, and impulsive children want to behave differently—they don't want to be in trouble all the time—but, despite their best efforts, they can't modify their behavior even if doing so would obtain them a valued reward.

Another frustrating component of ADHD is illustrated by the following example:

After years of chasing her son around and trying to teach him to "behave," Christine brought her seven-year-old son, Ethan, to the family pediatrician for an evaluation. Ethan was literally kicking and screaming as she drove him there. In the waiting room he disturbed several other patients by sliding picture books across the floor and under their chairs. Finally, Christine ended up with her rather sizable boy squirming around on her lap. When they were finally led back to the consulting room and both mom and son took their seats, the doctor asked about the reason for their visit. By this time, Christine was nearly beside herself, she was flushed and began ranting about Ethan's extreme misbehavior while Ethan sat still and looked up at the doctor with his big, beautiful, brown eyes. After a few minutes, the doctor asked to visit alone with Ethan. Five minutes later, he invited Christine back into the consulting room and informed her that Ethan seemed to him to be a calm, polite, and well-adjusted boy. Christine's reaction was so vigorous that, before she left, the doctor offered *her* a prescription for a tranquilizing medication!

Granted, the preceding example is extreme, but it clearly illustrates two important facts about children with ADHD symptoms. First, when in new and stimulating situations, a child with ADHD may not display the usual symptoms. No one knows why this is true. It might be because novel situations bring enough stimulation to calm their minds and bodies. The frontal lobe of the brain—the portion of the brain that's thought to be underactive in ADHD children—might be getting a neurochemical boost from interesting and engaging situations. This also might explain why ADHD children often can focus for long periods on highly interactive and stimulating video games.

Second, children with ADHD also often calm down and work well in one-on-one situations—especially if the situation or the people involved are new and interesting. They have a much more difficult time in school or other group situations where polite or proper behavior is required in a group context, and little one-on-one attention is available. This big contrast in behavior can make you think you're raising two different children.

More Ways You Can Help Your Child

Even though there is no cure, ADHD can be managed. Through specific parenting and classroom strategies, symptoms can be controlled to some extent. These same strategies are useful with children who don't have an ADHD diagnosis but are strong-willed, high-energy, or distractible.

Take a look at the list of home remedies or "Helpful Hints" for helping a child with ADHD. Remember, when it comes to managing behavior problems of ADHD children, parents and teachers are key players.

Helpful Hints for Your Child's ADHD

➤ Families First, a parent education organization, has a philosophy toward children that bears repeating. When children misbehave, they tell parents to "Get Curious, Not Furious!" Parents of active, impulsive, or inattentive children should heed this recommendation. Before taking action, explore reasons why your child is behaving the way he's behaving. Then respond thoughtfully.

➤ ADHD or ADHD-like children need rules and limits. They are often unable to manage their own behaviors and so they need wise and prudent adults to help them do so. Establish rules and also small and reasonable consequences for breaking the rules. Then follow through, over and over.

➤ Plan ahead, and then plan some more. For example, when there's going to be required sedentary time, as in long car trips, plan many stops, activities, music, headphones, rewards for good behavior, and so on.

➤ When possible and when appropriate, accommodate. Give your busy child lots of roaming room. Give the distractible child small tasks.

> ➤ Give your attention to the child when he's behaving acceptably and, if possible, ignore him and reduce his fun when he's misbehaving.

> ➤ Be ready to respond positively to desirable behavior at a moment's notice. When the high-energy child manages to settle down for a minute or two, notice, and have a little treat ready if it's appropriate. When the distracted child finishes a task, be sure to notice, hug, and occasionally give him a surprise reward.

> ➤ Be encouraging. This is especially important because your child is probably not getting positive encouragement from others. Say "I know you can do it!" or "It will feel so good when you get that homework done!" Make other statements that let your child know you believe in his abilities.

> ➤ Give clear, repeated instructions in chunks the size your child can absorb. Don't deliver long lectures. Instead, deliver short sound bites and then check to see if your child understood the instructions by having him repeat them back to you.

> ➤ Because your child will do better if he has your close, personal attention, plan plenty of one-on-one time with him, if possible.

> ➤ Turn off the television and limit the computer/video games. You're the parent and the boss. Especially make these restrictions if you're expecting or hoping for your child to actually absorb the things you're saying.

If your child has ADHD, his behavior probably overwhelms you—at least sometimes. Therefore, we strongly recommend that you look for and find support for yourself. This support may come in the form of a regular baby-sitter, time away from your child, counseling for yourself, or plenty of opportunities for exercise. It's of the utmost importance for you to take care of your own health and sanity when facing a challenging family situation.

Summing It Up

As you probably know, living with a child who has ADHD symptoms is frustrating and challenging. Even though ADHD is a very common problem, its exact cause and cure are still unknown. If you think your child has ADHD, take him to a professional for an evaluation and possibly treatment, as soon as possible. Although many parents are comfortable giving their children medication to manage ADHD symptoms, others are not. We recommend that you try using positive, nondrug approaches first. You can always try medications later, in combination with nondrug approaches. We also recommend that you learn everything you can about ADHD and that you find yourself support for dealing with a very difficult situation.

Check It Out

Attention-Deficit/Hyperactivity Disorder by Larry B. Silver (Washington, DC: American Psychiatric Association, 1998). Here you'll find a comprehensive and traditional medical perspective on ADHD, including strategies for managing and treating this challenging condition.

Brainstorms: Understanding and Treating the Emotional Storms of ADHD from Childhood through Adulthood by H. Joseph Horacek (Northvale, NJ: Jason Aronson, 2000). If you want to read about ADHD from an author who also identifies ADHD symptoms in many prominent historical figures such as Albert Einstein and Amelia Earhart, try this book.

The Myth of the ADD Child by Thomas Armstrong (New York: Penguin, 1995). This alternative, nonmedical approach emphasizes positive qualities associated with ADHD and tries to protect children and families from the negative effects of psychiatric labeling.

Power Parenting for Children with ADD/ADHD by Grad Flick (Hoboken, NJ: Jossey-Bass, 1996). This practical book can help you establish a behavioral modification program for your challenging child.

Raising Your Spirited Child: A Guide for Parents Whose Child Is More Intense, Sensitive, Perceptive, Persistent, Energetic by Mary Sheedy Kurcinka (New York: HarperPerennial, 1992). There are many books for parents with children who misbehave but who do not really meet the criteria for ADHD. Most of the parents we work with rate Kurcinka's book as the most helpful.

Taking Charge of ADHD: The Complete, Authoritative Guide for Parents by Russell A. Barkley (New York: Guilford Press, 2000). This is another good source for understanding the traditional medical perspective.

Talking Back to Ritalin: What Doctors Aren't Telling You About Stimulants and ADHD by Peter R. Breggin (New York: Perseus Publishing, 1998). Breggin offers another, more radical, nonmedical approach.

Chapter 5

Ups & Downs: Problems with Moods

> I did not know what to say to him. I felt awkward and blundering. I did not know how I could reach him, where I could overtake him and go on hand in hand with him once more. It is such a secret place, the land of tears.
> **—Antoine de Saint-Exupéry, *The Little Prince***

Looking in from the outside, an adult (with a bad memory) might think of childhood as a carefree time, with little responsibility and few worries. The reality is quite different. Childhood is a time of rapid physical, mental, and emotional change—a constant challenge. As suggested in the opening quote from *The Little Prince*, deep feelings of sadness are part of every child's experience at times, and these feelings are often quite private and difficult for parents to reach. When your child is crying or seems down in the dumps, it's really hard to know whether she's just experiencing normal sadness or something more extreme, something out of the ordinary.

One of our daughters has her own particular way of dealing with sad or upsetting situations. She cries. And then she begins to sob. And then she has trouble catching her breath and begins sputtering as she tries talking about what's wrong. What we've discovered about this daughter is that her entire body becomes caught up in her sadness and despair. She feels things and expresses herself deeply and powerfully. For her, a good cry—or rather a big cry—seems healthy and cleansing. She almost always feels better after letting out her sad feelings, especially if we can hang in there with her and share the experience, which isn't always easy.

It's hard to imagine that until the early 1970s, most parents, and even most mental health professionals, didn't recognize that children had the psychological capacity to be seriously depressed. We now know that children can indeed experience much more than passing sadness; like adults, they can experience a diagnosable condition usually referred to as clinical depression. Even more important for us parents to remember is that children's moods and reactions can be quite different from the normal moods and reactions of adults. Your child's mood problems need to be understood from a child's perspective.

For the last couple of months, Ellen stayed in bed longer than anyone else in the family, and her parents were growing concerned. When they woke her, even if it was early afternoon, she was extremely grouchy and snapped at them for bothering her. Often, they reacted by scolding her. Then she cried and said she was sorry, but that she just didn't feel like getting up or like talking to them. Sometimes, she stayed in her room all day if no one made her come out.

When this first started, Ellen's parents thought perhaps sleeping in late on Saturdays was just typical early adolescent behavior. She occasionally stayed up really late on Friday night, reading or watching videos. However, as her parents began to worry, they watched her sleep patterns more closely and noticed that even when Ellen got to bed early, she didn't get up easily. About the same time the sleep patterns changed, Ellen's appetite disappeared. She picked at her food, claiming it didn't taste very good. She said she was too tired to do much homework, practice piano, or even play games with her siblings—something she used to love to do.

※ ↗↙↗↙↖ ↙↗ ▪

Tu, a sixth-grader whose parents had emigrated to the United States from Laos, was a source of worry for his teachers. He was a very bright, motivated student, and until a couple months ago, he'd been outgoing, happy, and easy to get along with. However, more recently, he was withdrawn and irritable to the point of actually telling off his gym teacher and getting an in-school suspension. He stopped turning in homework, sat sullen and withdrawn from everyone in class, and snapped at people who used to be his friends.

When Tu's parents were contacted, they said things had become difficult at home as well. He had always been a boy who cared a great deal for his younger siblings and his parents, but now he was behaving disrespectfully, ignoring his younger brothers and sisters, and refusing to help with his usual chores. They were very worried, but didn't know where to turn.

※ ↗↙↗↙↖ ↙↗ ▪

Although Ellen and Tu behaved differently, they were both showing distinct and dramatic shifts from their usual way of being; their general mood, motivation levels, appetites, and attitudes changed. If your child has significant changes in her behavior, you may be unsure how to interpret the changes. Does growing up just bring these changes? Is it just a passing thing, caused by a failed test or cruel treatment by friends? If everyone in the family just ignores the changes, will they go away? In this chapter we'll explore what's normal and what's not when it comes to your child's moods. We'll also briefly focus on the difficult issue of youth suicide. Even though it can be scary to take a close look at your child's moods and potential self-destructive behavior, reading this chapter will make it easier for you to help your child through these problems.

What Is Mood?

It's probably a safe bet to assume that—at least once—your child has been in a bad *mood*. The word *mood* can refer to either your child's temporary emotional state, resulting from good or bad events in the day, or to a more constant feeling or emotional state. *Mood* is also used by both parents and children to refer to a wide variety of feelings; your child, for example, may be in a silly mood, an irritable mood, or a good or bad mood. Another term, *mood disorder*, is used by mental health professionals to refer to serious problems with moods such as depression, mania, and marked swings between the two.

Understanding Depression

Depression, like *mood*, is a commonly used term. Most of us say "I'm depressed" at some time or another. The word is often used to mean a general, but temporary, condition of feeling down, sad, or dejected. Virtually everyone experiences this sort of normal depression. It can come after being turned down for a date or a raise, missing a favorite television show, or hearing about upsetting world or family events— or it can seem to come out of the blue.

Clinical Depression

This normal depression—having down feelings that come and go from time to time—is not the same as the more serious *clinical depression* that is diagnosed by mental health professionals in both adults and children. Children with clinical depression experience a group of symptoms that are present most of the day—on more days than not, and that directly cause them distress or interfere with their going to school, playing sports, making friends, or other normal activities. Clinical depression is much more than a temporary down time.

The following list of possible depression symptoms can help you determine if your child has problems serious enough to consider seeking professional help. This list is adapted from the American Psychiatric Association's *Diagnostic and Statistical Manual of Mental Disorders* (also known as DSM—see page 22).

Signs of a Serious Problem with Depression

❏ My child is either very sad or very irritable most of the day and nearly every day. She has told me so or I've observed it (or another adult has). My child doesn't shown much emotion— she doesn't laugh or smile at jokes or other things that used to delight her.

❏ My child has become much less interested in the activities that usually make her happy. Or she reports little pleasure or satisfaction in these activities. She isolates herself—with television, computer games, video games, or other individual activities.

❏ My child's appetite has vastly increased or decreased, and that change is apparent nearly every day. Or, my child has either lost or gained more than five percent of her body weight, or she has failed to make normal and expected weight gains associated with childhood growth.

❏ My child has begun sleeping too much or too little nearly every day.

❏ My child is either worked up and agitated or slowed down nearly every day. I can tell by watching her. My child's irritability and agitation sometimes involves blatant meanness toward other children, adults, or objects.

❏ My child seems excessively tired or has very little energy nearly every day.

❑ My child acts or talks like she's worthless or like she has low self-esteem. She also talks a lot about how bad or guilty she feels about things. She refers to herself with negative descriptions such as useless, dumb, stupid, or ugly.

❑ My child's ability to think clearly, concentrate, or make decisions has gotten worse.

❑ My child has repeating thoughts about death, suicide, suicide attempts, or has a specific plan for committing suicide.

Although it's not included in the DSM, the following symptom is not unusual as a possible indicator of childhood depression:

❑ My child regularly complains of non-migraine headaches, abdominal pain, or other body aches and pains (not just associated with refusal to attend school).

Is It Depression, Grief, or Normal Moodiness?

It's very hard to know for sure, without consulting a professional, whether your child is *really* depressed, or whether she's just experiencing a normal, temporary down period of childhood. As a first step, here's a good general guideline: if your child has been showing at least five of the ten characteristics listed in the previous depression checklist more or less steadily for over two weeks, she may be experiencing a form of clinical depression commonly known as *major depression.* However, before you worry too much about your child's possible depression, you should also consider the following issues.

Keep in mind that many other childhood conditions or situations can cause your child to look depressed. For example, children whose parents have died often seem depressed but are only going through normal bereavement. Normal bereavement involves the same symptoms as depression, but a medical diagnosis of depression would not be given unless the symptoms persist for at least two months after the death or loss of a loved one, because children need time to recover from this very sad event. If your child has recently lost a loved one, you should make sure she has plenty of opportunities to talk with someone, including you, about her feelings. She may also benefit from grief counseling, a grief group for children (some schools, faith communities, community programs, and mental health professionals offer these), or from alternative ways of expressing her sadness and pain, perhaps through drawing, writing, or storytelling (see pages 125–126 for more information on this).

For many parents, the concept of childhood depression is confusing and frustrating. After all, many children are naturally very sensitive and moody. Other children, like our daughter mentioned earlier, will express their sadness with such drama that it seems like there must be some sort of horrible underlying problem. Still other children may quietly suffer from insomnia, deep sadness, loss of appetite, and even suicidal thinking, without ever telling anyone. Also, if it's present in your child only briefly, depression is mostly normal and your child will bounce back to her old happy self without too much trouble.

Perhaps the best remedy to all this confusion about depression in children is for you to know your child well and watch her closely. Be aware that, more than anything, depression in your child will be a change from happier times. It's important for you to be the kind of parent who will notice—and try to help with—longer-lasting mood changes in your child.

Dysthymia—Another Form of Depression

In addition to major depression, described earlier, there is another form of depression called *dysthymic disorder* or *dysthymia*. Dysthymia is generally less severe, but lasts longer than major depression. People suffering from dysthymia often describe themselves as feeling "down in the dumps" almost all the time. In children, dysthymia may appear as almost constant irritability.

Signs of a Serious Problem with Mild, Long-Term Depression

❑ My child is in a very unhappy or irritable mood most of the day and more days than not.

❑ My child usually has a poor appetite or is frequently overeating.

❑ My child regularly sleeps too much or not enough (one or the other, not both).

❑ My child has low energy or seems tired all the time.

❏ My child has low self-esteem.

❏ My child has trouble concentrating or has lots of difficulty making decisions

❏ My child talks about feelings of hopelessness about the future.

If your child has this more mild, but longer-term form of depression, what you'll see is an unhappy or irritable mood plus at least two other symptoms on this list. All these symptoms must be present for at least a year for dysthmia to be diagnosed. If your child had a month or two during the past year when things were better, but overall your child had far more irritable and down months than not, then the diagnosis of dysthmia might still be appropriate.

What's Causing Your Child's Depression?

If you could put your finger on the cause of your child's depression, that might make it easier for you. But no one really knows exactly what causes depression. In many cases, depression seems to show up in direct response to a life event, such as school failure, physical or sexual abuse, or when parents divorce. On the other hand, major depression also may have strong genetic or biological underpinnings. Biogenetic explanations for depression are probably more likely when depressive symptoms start very early, are relatively severe, and when there are no clear situational reasons why your child has become depressed.

Considering Your Child's Age and Temperament

Research has shown that depressed children do show a slightly different set of reactions and symptoms than adults. Certainly, they might be sad, have trouble with sleeping, eating, and concentrating, and show reduced interest in pleasurable activities—just like adults, but they're also likely to complain more often of frequent headaches or stomachaches, act abysmally grouchy or irritable, become socially withdrawn, or express an exaggerated "I don't care" attitude.

Overall, it's fairly rare for very young children to become clinically depressed. Mild or intermittent sadness, irritability, sleep problems, and other signs of depression are a part of normal childhood experiences. Usually, if your child is really displaying signs of depression, she'll be experiencing a major upheaval in her daily life.

Only about two to five percent of preadolescent children report mild to moderate depressive symptoms.

However, as adolescence hits, depression rates go up considerably. There are many reasons for this increase. These reasons include hormonal changes, greater ability to think about life in the future and imagine terrible outcomes, less satisfying relationships with parents, body changes (including, but not limited to, the almighty pimple), and having mean and inconsistent teenagers as friends.

From a parent's perspective, one very hopeful thing about depression in children is that it tends to be very temporary. Even if your child becomes depressed, she's likely to recover with or without formal treatment. In fact, in one study, 69 percent of depressed children who were given a placebo—a very small sugar pill—recovered from their depressive symptoms within four to six weeks! This information might cause you to wonder if you should even consider taking your child for treatment for depression; after all, why not just wait for the depression to lift, as it's likely to do in the majority of cases? But consider this: Although childhood depression almost always goes away, if your child doesn't receive treatment, she'll suffer from her miserable symptoms longer and be more likely to experience repeated and increasingly worse bouts of depression in the future.

Getting Professional Help

The bad news about childhood depression is that it's absolutely miserable and can make it extremely hard for your child to function at home and at school. The good news about childhood depression, as mentioned earlier, is that it's usually a temporary condition and the symptoms often will go away, especially if your child receives psychological counseling.

A ten-year-old child named Wesley was referred for counseling because he was crying almost every day after school. Not surprisingly, his parents were extremely upset and puzzled. And because he didn't seem able to tell them why he was so upset, they were considering antidepressant medication treatment. However, through play and the use of puppets in a few counseling sessions, Wesley was able to describe how he was feeling and to reveal that a school bully was picking on him, rather viciously, at recess every day. After that discovery, Wesley and his counselor were able to make a plan for dealing with the bully, a plan that included telling his parents and enlisting the aid of his school principal. Of course, the problem with the bully didn't go away immediately (bullies are like that), but over time, Wesley felt better and better about ways that he and important adults in his life were able to deal with his difficult situation.

tz ztzzzzzw/zzo-m

Although approaches to counseling depressed children vary considerably, counselors should regularly involve you in the counseling or inform you about what's happening in counseling. With children around ten and younger, most counselors will use a combination of play and talk to help children cope with difficult situations more effectively, as with Wesley and the bully. Sometimes, rather than begin therapy with a young child, a counselor may decide to meet with you to help you have more positive and constructive ways of parenting your child.

Depression and the Brain

Some professionals refer to depression as a *chemical imbalance* in the brain. This statement is at best oversimplified, and at worst, misleading. The human brain is an amazing organ. All brain functioning—thinking, remembering, regulating, feeling, and so on—involves exceedingly complex interactions of chemicals (called *neurochemicals* in the brain) and electrical impulses. Scientists simply don't know what a chemically or electrically *balanced* brain looks like. When your child is angry, her brain is chemically different than when she's happy. When she learns a new language, this language is stored chemically and electrically in her brain. Simply learning something new changes the chemical balance in her brain. The substances your child eats and drinks temporarily change the chemical balance in her brain—and thus change her moods, if only briefly. Exercise, too, changes brain chemistry, as does the experience of winning or losing a competitive sporting event. And of course, the way your child thinks and what she thinks about change her brain chemically—which may be why counseling can make such a difference in many cases.

Is Medication the Answer?

Many medications change brain chemistry in one way or another, but there are hundreds of neurochemicals that brain researchers have yet to understand. Currently, medications that increase the level of a neurochemical called *serotonin* within the brain are extremely popular. These serotonin-specific medications (such as Prozac, Zoloft, and Paxil) are prescribed for depression and also for such other problems as anxiety, migraine headaches, premenstrual difficulties, and post-traumatic stress disorder.

Oddly, such antidepressant medications haven't been shown to be very effective for most children. Currently, the U.S. Food and Drug Administration (FDA) has not approved any antidepressant medications for use with depressed children. No one really knows why depressed children don't have a clear, consistent, and positive response to antidepressant medications, but they don't.

Even though the FDA has not approved the use of antidepressant medications for depression in children, many physicians still prescribe them, sometimes because there seems to be no other alternative. Additionally, many mental health professionals have repeated clinical experiences where antidepressant medications seem to help individual children, and so there's a possibility that some children may have a positive response to medication treatment. However, overall, because counseling can be quite effective—and because the effects of these medications and their side effects on developing children aren't fully understood—it makes sense to try counseling before trying medications for children who are depressed. And, many physicians who prescribe these medications believe that they're most effective when paired with counseling.

More Ways You Can Help Your Child

While the terms *major depression* and *dysthymia* are specific psychiatric diagnoses, many children suffer from minor depressive symptoms that don't require professional help. What can you do to help your moody, crabby, or sad child? How can you prevent your child who may be mildly or intermittently depressed or prone to depression from getting even more clinically depressed? Consider the following "Helpful Hints for Your Child's Depression."

Helpful Hints for Your Child's Depression

➤ One of the greatest antidepressant activities available to adults and children is physical exercise. Of course, the last thing that depressed or crabby kids want to do is go out and get exercise. Refuse to take no for an answer. Give your child choices, "Would you like to come with me for a walk, do some yoga exercises with me, or do some aerobic dancing for the next 20 minutes ... take your pick!" Make regular exercise a consistent part of your child's life.

➤ A 30-minute therapeutic massage twice a week can reduce depression and anxiety, improve sleep patterns, lower stress hormone levels, and improve eating habits among children. The cool thing about this is that the massages can be administered by parents or grandparents.

➤ Maintaining a regular, healthy diet is crucial to good health and general well-being. Your mother or dad was right, and so are you when you say, "Eat your vegetables!" Too much sugar or caffeine adversely affects mood and other workings of the brain.

➤ Give your child positive feedback (five compliments to every criticism). By being a positive and supportive parent, you can help with your child's mood problems.

➤ Just because your child is moody and crabby, don't let that prevent you from requiring her to contribute to the household. Children prone to depression need to uphold their responsibilities such as doing chores, because doing so is good for their self-esteem.

➤ Spend time playing with your child. Sometimes your child may start thinking that you don't care for her or love her. By taking time to get on the floor and play, you're showing interest and giving attention in a way that can't help but be seen as loving and caring.

➤ There is great wisdom in the following four words: This too shall pass. Children need help realizing that time passes and things change, often for the better. Talking positively and reassuringly about the future helps.

➤ Bad moods, sad moods, and depression are linked to the way we think. We can think ourselves into very bad moods, and by changing the ways we think, and what we think about, we can change our mood. Helping children learn to think more optimistically can help them manage their moods. However, be gentle, because no one likes to be told to "cheer up and look at the bright side of life."

➤ Listening to an irritable child can be a chore. It's hard not to let the irritability get contagious. But listening all the way through a grumpy story can help because talking about feelings is healthier, both physically and emotionally, than holding feelings inside. On the other hand, just because your child is grumpy and irritable, doesn't mean you have to always sit and listen to her. Instead, what's important is a balance; take some time to listen carefully to your child's feelings, but at other times it's perfectly fine to let your child know that a discussion of her negative feelings has to wait ... or has to end.

➤ Giving your child space to work things out is also important. Some children need time alone to get their bearings.

➤ Depressed children often have depressed parents. If you tend to be depressed, work on dealing with your own situation, so you can be a healthier, more positive parent.

Understanding Mania

Mania refers to an abnormally positive or irritable mood, accompanied by lots and lots of overactivity. People who are manic often become completely delusional, getting out of touch with reality. For example, in our counseling practice, we've worked with manic patients who believed they were President of the United States, Jesus Christ, and a member of the Seattle Supersonics basketball team.

In adults, mania is extremely disturbing and extremely debilitating. Frequently, manic moods alternate with severe depression; this condition, one that includes extreme mood swings, is officially referred to as *bipolar disorder*. Among children, mania and bipolar disorder are fairly rare. Some professionals believe that preadolescent children can have early onset bipolar disorder, but this perspective is still being researched. Bipolar disorder is more likely to appear in children with a strong family history of the condition.

If your child has mania, she's likely to believe she can accomplish nearly anything. She talks or moves around nonstop, rarely sleeps, and bounces around the house like a rubber ball. Obviously, this description is very similar to the description of children with ADHD in Chapter 4, and you'll probably need to visit a professional to tell whether your child has ADHD or mania. Usually, if your child is in a manic state, she's likely to be:

- sleeping very little
- making—and believing—extremely positive and unrealistic statements ("I'm the queen, I can fly, I'm a millionaire")
- behaving so disruptively that it's impossible to do anything else in your household but manage her behavior
- showing irritability, aggressiveness, or anger ("Get away from me, I'm busy!")
- cycling back and forth between extreme sadness and extreme happiness, sometimes even during a single day
- behaving so disruptively that it's impossible to do anything else in your household but manage her behavior

Lisa, an eleven-year-old girl, was brought to us for counseling by her parents who were worried because in the past four months, she had developed severe mood swings. She had also stayed up all night four or five times, prowling the house, cleaning, cooking things, and practicing piano. If her parents tried to get her to go to bed, she responded so angrily, they just backed off. After these all-nighters, Lisa insisted on going to school, and actually made it through the day without falling asleep. However, she was terribly irritable, demanding, and out of control both at home and at school. Consequently, Lisa was referred for a psychiatric evaluation and put on a carefully managed dosage of mood-stabilizing medication. We also worked with Lisa's family on the many important aspects of managing this kind of problem.

+12711w710m

While there's still much to learn about bipolar disorder in children, it has become much more commonly diagnosed in the past few years. If your child experiences extreme and dangerous mood swings, especially when there is no clear reason for these changes, quickly consult with a mental health professional who works with children with severe psychological disorders.

Suicidal or Self-Destructive Impulses

Suicidal thoughts and feelings are very often related to depression or bipolar disorder. Suicide is extremely rare for preadolescent children, but devastating when it occurs. Therefore, we've listed some common

"Signs of a Serious Problem with Suicidal Thoughts." These are warning signs of suicide—take them seriously.

Signs of a Serious Problem with Suicidal Thoughts

❏ My child has made a direct suicide threat ("I'm just gonna kill myself.")

❏ My child has made an indirect suicide threat ("I wish I was dead.")

❏ My child seems especially focused on death in drawings, stories, poems, or her play.

❏ My child has shown a dramatic change in her personality or appearance.

❏ My child is overwhelmed with guilt, shame, or rejection.

❏ My child has just had a severe drop in school performance.

❏ My child is giving or throwing away important possessions.

❏ My child has been in possession of a dangerous weapon.

❏ My child has had an unexplained surge of cheerfulness or energy following a prolonged period of depression.

If you observe any of the suicide warning signs on the checklist, it's definitely time to do something. Unfortunately, because every child and situation is unique, it can be hard to know exactly the right thing to do. Several tips are offered in the "Helpful Hints for Your Child's Suicidal Thoughts" list.

At certain ages, children seem more prone to talk about suicidal impulses. For example, for whatever reason, ten-year-old boys talk about suicide—usually as a symptom of their discontent with home or school life—at a rate higher than girls at this age or children at other ages.

Helpful Hints for Your Child's Suicidal Thoughts

➤ Find a way to ask about suicide (asking won't increase suicide risk; not asking may increase risk, because if you don't know what your child's thinking, you can't help).

➤ Listen to your child. Avoid rushing into reassurance ("Oh, you'll feel better soon!"). Give your full attention. Don't rush to pass judgment or to give advice.

➤ Express your love and concern. Do this in meaningful ways that have touched your child in the past.

➤ Help your child with problem-solving. Depression and suicidal thoughts often happen when a person doesn't see any other alternatives to feeling miserable. Therefore, acknowledge that suicide is a possible option, but talk about other options as well.

➤ Tell your child that thoughts of suicide and helplessness are part of depression. Then let her know that young people can be helped with their depressed feelings and so that is a reasonable option to check out before pursuing suicide.

➤ Stay with your child. Isolation contributes to suicide.

➤ Ask your child to go with you to see a counselor, minister, or whatever professional person she's willing to see. Let your child choose who to see, but not whether to see someone for help.

➤ Reduce the risk by taking away the means. Lock away guns or give them to someone for safekeeping. You also may need to securely store medications, poisons, and ropes.

➤ Let your child know how much he or she means to you. Never let your child doubt your love. Make an effort to do fun things with your child.

➤ Ask your child to promise not to hurt herself or try suicide. If she won't make a no-suicide promise, consider hospitalization.

Whenever your child talks or acts in ways that reflect death or self-destructiveness, even in jest or manipulation, take time to check in with your child and try to understand what has prompted this sort of thinking and behavior. Talk with your child about her fears and disappointments, and help her see that threatening or wishing for death isn't a good solution. If, after talking, you still have concerns, call a mental health professional and discuss the problem as soon as possible. If your child ever makes an actual attempt at suicide, depending on the severity of the attempt, take her to the hospital emergency room or immediately schedule a therapy appointment with a licensed mental health professional.

Sometimes, children burn or cut themselves on purpose, but without intending to kill themselves. In mid- to late adolescence, many children become interested in body piercing, tattoos, and even branding for fashion and peer acceptance reasons. While some parents object to these activities, they are not, in themselves, signs of emotional disturbance. However, slicing one's arms and burning one's skin with hot objects or cigarettes are not done for the sake of peer-approved fashion. Self-injurious behaviors such as these are more serious and signal that your child is experiencing inner turmoil. As with suicide attempts, if children cause themselves bodily harm, it's time for professional help.

Summing It Up

Until the early 1970s, it was believed that children weren't able to experience depression. We know now that children can, and do, become depressed and need professional help. Clinical depression involves more than a sad mood. Eating and sleeping habits change. Attitudes toward friends and activities change. If your child appears severely depressed for over two weeks or mildly depressed for over one year, take her to a physician or mental health professional for an evaluation.

Children may also experience manic episodes and develop bipolar disorder. Also, in extreme cases, children with depression or bipolar disorder may try to harm themselves or attempt suicide. If your child is very depressed or shows the symptoms of bipolar disorder, do everything you can to insure her safety.

Check It Out

The Bipolar Child: The Definitive and Reassuring Guide to Childhood's Most Misunderstood Disorder by Demitri Papolos and Janice Papolos (New York: Broadway Books, 1999). This recent and popular book on bipolar or "manic-depressive" illness in children provides parents and professionals with a glimpse of what early onset bipolar disorder looks like in very young children (as young as five years old).

"Help Me, I'm Sad" by David Fassler and Lynne S. Dumas (New York: Viking Penguin, 1998). Here's a basic book on childhood depression written from the psychiatric perspective.

The Optimistic Child by Martin E.P. Seligman (New York: HarperCollins, 1995). Learn more about the way children's thinking can affect their mood. Seligman, past president of the American Psychological Association, also helps teachers, parents, and other child caregivers to see that there are other ways than false praise to rebuild our children's self-esteem, including skill-building and tolerating failure.

When Nothing Matters Anymore by Bev Cobain (Minneapolis: Free Spirit Publishing, 1998). This award-winning book is excellent for children who are soon-to-be adolescents. The author, cousin of the famous rock star Kurt Cobain, who tragically committed suicide, explores her own pain at his loss, and the wish that he could have obtained the help he needed. She describes the causes and types of depression, then discusses different kinds of treatment, how they help, and how to stay healthy.

Chapter 6

Getting Along: Problems with Sexual Development and Social Skills

"Splendid, splendid, splendid," exclaimed the Whether Man. "Whether or not you find your own way, you're bound to find some way. If you happen to find my way, please return it, as it was lost years ago. I imagine right now it's quite rusty. . . ."
—**Norton Juster, The Phantom Tollbooth**

If you spend a few minutes with a group of kids on a playground or at a party, you'll notice one thing right away—children don't always get along famously. Some of them have a few rough social edges; they're bossy, mean, passive, and sometimes, much to their parent's dismay, they're a bit odd. A complaint we often hear from parents is: "Why can't my son (or daughter) just get along with the other kids?"

When it comes to children's social skills, there are wide variations— even charmingly refreshing variations—in what's normal. When a twelve-year-old boy at a concert we attended began gyrating to the music, girls giggled and parents chuckled, but this boy, complete with hair flying and hips swaying, was accepted for being a quirky but enthusiastic music enthusiast. His actions prompted amusement, not concern. At the same concert, however, we saw a girl who never said hello or uttered a single word to anyone there. Her actions might call for concerned attention from a caring adult in her life.

Of course, there isn't one best way to be. Your child needs to find his *own* way, not just some way. But he may need help to learn how to make his own social style work. If he gets completely derailed, he may need lots of help from you and others to get back on track.

Children need clear adult guidance in the area of sexual development. We'll say much more about sex and sexuality as this chapter proceeds, but for now: be forewarned! Some material in this chapter, because it's so straightforward and explicit, may cause you discomfort. For many of us, talking about sex with children and even *reading* about talking about sex with children can bring up strong feelings. Nonetheless, rather than dance around these challenging issues, we've decided to take a very direct approach to talking about children's sexual development. Our goal is not to offend, but to openly address real-life sexual issues that you and your child may face.

Sometimes, Katie, a petite seven-year-old, would jump into her mother's arms, and with others present, poke at her mother's breasts and say embarrassing things, such as "You sure have big tits, Mommy." Katie's mother, Gloria, was very embarrassed by this odd behavior, and really didn't like the words Katie used. Gloria was sure Katie picked up this behavior at her cousin's house, but when it came to responding to Katie, she was speechless. Katie had also begun asking difficult questions about men, women, sex, and anatomy. She also wanted to bathe with Gloria, and would often run around the house naked, sometimes with her fingers in her vagina. Because Katie's father lived in another state, and saw Katie very infrequently, Gloria felt very alone in facing this problem.

⁓⁓⁓⁓⁓⁓

Sameep was an active, happy, nine-year-old who loved to tease and pester girls. At school, he lifted their skirts, got other boys to chase girls with him, and sometimes embarrassed them by shouting out words like bitch, or even worse anatomical slang words (which we'll leave to your imagination). Occasionally, Sameep got into a bit of trouble here and there, but nothing very extensive. Then, one afternoon, he got caught in the girl's bathroom with his pants down.

The school called Sameep's parents to let them know about Sameep's behavior and the consequences, which included after-school detention. They also suggested that Sameep's parents consider getting him some counseling. Sameep's father, Dario, was sure the school was overreacting, and the thought of counseling didn't fit with his religious views. "Boys will be boys," he said. However, in contrast to Dario's reaction, Sameep's mother wasn't so sure that her son was behaving like a normal boy.

⁓⁓⁓⁓⁓⁓

Third-grader Mandy was a handful-and-a-half for her busy parents. Mandy had some rather particular interests and she stubbornly hung on to her preferences, regardless of anything her parents said. For example, she insisted on wearing sweats and high-top basketball shoes to school every day. And she usually kept her jacket on all day as well. Mandy often refused to take showers and frequently claimed, "I hate taking stupid showers!" She also resisted getting her hair cut or styled, and if she played with anyone at school, it was with a few boys who were quite immature for their age. Mandy's father had been very shy as a boy and so he was at a loss about whether Mandy's behavior was a problem or was just normal behavior. Mandy's mother was worried about Mandy's refusal to wear slacks, skirts, or even blue jeans and she couldn't help wondering if Mandy's stubbornness and unusual clothing selections might be why Mandy was never invited to play after school and never had anyone over.

Children's sexual and social development can be rocky for everyone involved. Parents often complain that sex is everywhere—it's used to sell shoes, cars, aftershave, and even chewing gum. It's also used for entertainment, and too often paired with violence and other undesirable behaviors.

Your child's sexual and social development has both physical and psychological aspects. In addition, you may have strong personal and family values about sexual and social topics. And if all that weren't enough, your child's sexual and social struggles will probably remind you of your own successes and failures in these areas. Most of us remember more than a few painful, or maybe even amazed, moments involving social embarrassment, "the facts of life," or the "birds and the bees." Because of this, you may be quite powerfully affected as your child encounters social and sexual milestones along the path toward adulthood.

Is What's Considered "Normal" Okay for Your Child?

A friend of ours has a daughter, Nikolia, who's in first grade. One morning Nikolia's mom called us in distress, dumbfounded by the fact that her daughter was "asked out" by a boy in her first-grade class. Our friend said, "I didn't think I'd have to deal with this for a few more years!" She explained that because she and her husband have strong Greek Orthodox views, they've decided their daughter won't "date" until age sixteen. She went on to say that she wouldn't be nearly so upset about the boy's behavior, but she'd learned the boy's father had encouraged his son to ask her daughter out to the movies. She said, "I can tell that seven-year-old boy my daughter's not going out with him, but what do I tell the father?"

As is the case with every topic in this book, normal is a relative term; sometimes it's hard to know what's normal, what's not, and what to do about it. For our friend and for many parents, the whole idea of what's normal and healthy social and sexual behavior is especially controversial. This is partly because social and sexual behavior choices are deeply personal, very different for different families, and often related to religious and cultural values. You may not agree with our Greek Orthodox friend's "no dating until age sixteen" rule, and you may not agree with everything we say in this chapter. Our purpose is to openly discuss sexual and social development and then let you decide how our discussion fits or doesn't fit your values. We commend every brave parent who finds ways to discuss these important issues at home.

In at least one more way, the concept of what's normal and what's acceptable takes on a slightly different tone in this chapter. One day, we came home from work and found our thirteen-year-old daughter watching TV after school. As we sat down to check in with her and check out the show, we were stunned to hear, at 4:15 P.M. on network television, the "couples" on this show talking about sadomasochism and orgies. As a consequence, one of us called the local station to complain, only to be informed that the show was scheduled to be in this "normal" time slot for the next six months.

The point is that, especially when it comes to social and sexual behavior, what's considered normal by some isn't always acceptable or good for children. As parents, you don't have to accept anything your child does just because it's typical for most children his age. In fact, you'll find that when your child tells you "but everybody's doing it!" that's a very good time to look closely at whatever he wants to be able to do and determine, for yourself—for your individual family—whether it's acceptable behavior, regardless of what all the other kids are doing.

Social Skills

All children need at least a few very basic social skills to get along in life. We're not talking about proper etiquette, like knowing which fork to use at dinner, but about practical skills to help them be comfortable and effective in their interactions with other people.

Considering Your Child's Age and Temperament

At a parenting class, a distraught dad recently told us, "My seven-year-old has to have her way or she just blows up at other kids. Yesterday, at school, when her classmates wouldn't do what she wanted, she jumped up and started kicking sand at them. That little incident got her a trip to the principal's office."

A mom in the class chimed in: "My boy is bossy, too. When I come by the playground, I usually see him off by himself, playing alone. It just breaks my heart to see that. I want so much for him to have friends—because I remember being alone myself when I was young. I ask him why he plays alone and he says, 'Everybody else is bossy. They won't play dinosaurs. So I play by myself.'"

One of the most practical and important social skills for your child to develop is this: the ability to play cooperatively with other children. If he isn't able to play cooperatively after age five or so, it's not a major cause for alarm. But it might mean he needs a little special coaching from you or from other adults or older children to help him develop this way of playing. Although some children seem to have this skill down at a very early age, others lag behind, sometimes for years. It's similar to learning to read or ride a bicycle; children vary dramatically in their social skill development.

Also, as you can see from the two examples of children who are bossy and want things *their* way, even children struggling with similar problems can do so in very different ways. The first child, when she doesn't get her way, responds with frustration and aggression (kicking sand). In contrast, the second child withdraws if other kids won't cooperate with what he wants to do. Remember, your child's social skills depend on:

- his temperament
- what he's learning from you and other family members
- what he's learning from peers and adults at school and in the neighborhood
- what he's learning from television and other media sources

Overall, your behavior is your child's most important teacher, so it's always a good idea, if your child has a problem with social skills, to consider how you act in similar situations, just in case he's following in your footsteps.

One of the most important social qualities to foster in your child is empathy. Empathy is the wonderful human attribute of being able to sense another person's joy or pain or worry and, importantly, being able to feel those emotions *with* the other person. Empathy development is what you're hoping for when you say "Now, how would *you* feel if someone did that to *you?*"

There's some evidence that children display empathy naturally at early ages. They might cry when they hear someone else crying. Two-year-olds have been known to offer their bottles to a sad-looking parent, or their crackers to an upset stranger. However, empathy is also taught. It's taught partly by example—so when children sense someone understands how they feel, and this feeling is mirrored back accurately, they not only feel loved and understood, they also learn to offer empathy to others.

Ironically, both shy and aggressive children lack empathy for others. Shy children have fears and internal turmoil that are so draining and distracting, they can't focus on what others are feeling. In contrast, aggressive children often focus on how unfair and mean others are being to them and then quickly respond with hostility and retaliation. Aggressive children usually don't understand the motives of others very well and don't trust the world to meet their needs. Learning the give-and-take necessary for healthy social relationships requires both empathy and some degree of self-confidence.

Children's social needs change drastically as they grow and mature. Your child can benefit from chances to interact socially with other children at very young ages. Play groups, even for toddlers, can help children learn how to get along. As your child gets older, he will begin to grow apart from you, and turn to peers for at least some of his social interactions, social validation, and recreation. However, he will engage in this process at his own rate, depending both on how close he feels to you, and on his own needs, interests, and temperament.

Adjusting Your Social Expectations

As parents, our expectations for our children's social behavior are frequently unrealistic. We often expect our two-year-olds to share toys with their friends, our four-year-olds to shake hands with adults, and our six-year-olds to nod their heads, make good eye contact, and look like they're listening when adults talk to them. The following guidelines are provided to help adjust your social expectations to meet your child's readiness.

Usually, two-year-olds don't share their toys. Sometimes four-year-olds have trouble sharing their toys as well. If your young child doesn't readily share or take turns, set up a system for that to happen ("You can each play with the train for five minutes"). Express empathy ("I can tell that sharing your toys feels hard for you right now"), but don't become overly concerned.

When meeting new people, especially adults, young children often pull away. It's unrealistic to expect handshakes or comments like "It was nice to meet you" until your child is age eight to ten. Feel free to tell your child what you'd like him to say because repetition and rehearsal help, but don't be too upset if it doesn't happen.

Many parents expect their children to display adult manners when eating meals at the table. Although you can teach table manners to fairly young children (about age six or so), they really don't have much positive motivation for this adult social behavior (which means that to get your child to behave at the dinner table may require threats, punishments, and other harsh behaviors on your part). Instead, it makes more sense to require brief (two- to five-minute) intervals of "good manners" and hold off on your big expectations until about age twelve, when your child begins to understand the positive consequences of having nice table manners.

Young children don't act at all like miniature adults; they often have poor listening and conversational skills, act self-centered when playing games, and ignore children who they've invited over to play. In other words, they often act like kids. For the most part, social skill development in children is so uneven and unpredictable until nearly puberty that it's best not to get too disturbed about your child's social miscues. If your expectations are too high, you'll just end up feeling frustrated, worried, and possibly angry about your child's social immaturity. Once again, we recommend that you let your child know what social behaviors you'd like to see, but try to be patient and nurturing as you watch them develop.

Troubling Behaviors and Recommended Responses

There may be very specific reasons why your child is struggling socially. In particular, be on the alert for bullying at school, problems at day care, mistreatment by a gym teacher, or other experiences that may be strongly affecting your child's social behavior. Addressing any threatening situations in your child's everyday world will help make it easier for him to be comfortable socially.

If your child's problems aren't too severe, simply having him become involved in social groups and projects can make a big difference in helping him learn social skills. Sports, hobbies, group lessons for art, language acquisition, writing, nature walks, can all be helpful. Parents need to not only provide the opportunity, but also provide incentives for becoming involved.

One very shy youngster we worked with was extremely resistant to the idea of joining the second-grade YMCA soccer team. Her parents, with our prompting, made a point to get to know the other team members, and made arrangements to carpool, including a stop for ice cream after practice with the other girls whenever they drove. This helped their daughter become better acquainted and more comfortable with the other little girls on the team.

Getting Professional Help

Children with serious social problems will need more than simple group opportunities to further their development. If a child is consistently miserable, or makes those around him miserable in most group settings, then he probably needs professional assistance. School counselors and others who work with children sometimes offer social skills training groups. Such groups are structured in ways to ensure that participating children are protected from mean-spirited interactions while they work on acquiring better social skills. If neither exposure to regular social groups, or attendance at professionally run social skills groups are possible, then you might want to pursue individual counseling for a child with major social problems.

Signs of a Serious Problem with Social Skills

❑ *Extreme shyness or lack of self-esteem.* My child has few or no friends. He hangs back and doesn't have, or refuses to use, the skills necessary to make social connections. He dreads social contact, is often tongue-tied, and finds others intimidating or frightening. He may be an easy target for bullying.

❏ *Bossy, rigid, controlling behaviors.* My child acts like he prefers to use people rather than relate to them. He always wants to play his favorite game and isn't interested in entertaining another point of view. If it can't go his way, he fights or quits. He seems to have no concept of give-and-take.

❏ *Selfish or self-centered.* My child avoids social contact primarily because he doesn't want someone else playing with his toys. He only wants to play if everyone pays attention to him, and if no one tries to steal the spotlight, eat some of his candy, or touch his things.

❏ *Bullying and meanness.* My child takes more delight in tormenting or making fun of other children than in playing cooperatively with them. He hasn't developed empathy, and uses force or cruel comments to hurt others and get his way.

❏ *Socially inept.* My child tries too hard. He pushes others away by being overeager. He talks too much, laughs too loud, clings tightly to would-be friends (even when the friend clearly wants to get away), and sometimes behaves foolishly to gain attention.

If you've checked any item listed on the "Signs of a Serious Problem with Social Skills" on pages 102–103, we recommend the following sequence of actions:

1. Have occasional chats with your child about the social behaviors you expect and hope for. Be very clear and positive and make sure he knows what you want. For example, you might say to your six-year-old son: "I've been concerned because you've been ignoring your friends when they come over to play. So, when Mario comes over today, I want you to say hello and play with him for at least 20 minutes. If you get tired of playing with him after that, just come to me and I can let him know it's time for him to go back to his home."

2. Be sure to closely examine your own social behavior. Sometimes our children are imitating things they see us do and we don't even realize it.

3. Closely watch your child to reduce the chances of his engaging in inappropriate social behavior. This doesn't mean you have to

hover over him like a helicopter, but try to be around so at least you know what's happening in the social arena.

4. Have a talk with your child's teachers or school counselors. They can let you know if your concerns are valid and if your expectations are reasonable. Ask if there is a social skills group for your child's age that he can join.

5. Consider taking a parenting class. Doing so can give you ideas to try out with your child. Parenting classes also can give you much needed support from other parents and help keep you from blaming yourself for your child's social struggles.

6. Call a child development or parenting specialist and have an informal chat about whether your expectations are on target. Your local mental health center, hospital, or college may be able to tell you how to reach such a specialist.

7. If the above steps have not resolved the problem, call and schedule an appointment with a counselor or psychologist for assessment and counseling, either for your child or to help you with parenting. Your child may feel shame and defensive about going to a counselor, assuming the problem is his fault, so it's a good idea to let him know that counseling isn't a punishment. Tell him it's a chance to sort things out and learn new things about the ways people get along.

Helpful Hints for Your Child's Social Problems

➤ Make sure your child has good hygiene. Children need to bathe almost daily and need reminders to brush their teeth, wear clean clothes, and comb their hair. You don't have to buy all the latest styles, but a few "cool" wardrobe items can go a long way in helping with self-esteem and peer acceptance.

➤ Insist on polite, respectful behavior at home, at least some of the time. Practice good manners. In our home, we like to declare on certain days that the Queen of England is visiting, and we practice how incredibly polite we would be if that were the case.

➤ Don't endorse, reward, or support aggressive, bullying behavior toward peers or younger children. If your child can't resolve his problems without becoming physical, that means he needs adult supervision and help resolving his conflicts.

➤ Try to instill empathy, both by modeling empathy yourself, and by encouraging your child to think (and feel) as if he were in someone else's shoes.

➤ Encourage shy children to give things a try. Do this in advance, so they know what you'd like them to try out and that you have confidence in their skills and abilities. In safe situations, you can even push them a little. For example, if you're going to visit a friend with a same-age child, you might say, "I want you to come over with me to Angelo's house while I talk with his mother. You can hang around me, but if he asks you to play, I want you to give it a try." Of course, it's important to avoid using shame or negative criticism when your child has social problems. He's probably already feeling ashamed and self-critical, and your negative comments will only compound the problem. Give your child lots and lots of support through hugs, pats on the back, and positive feedback.

➤ Invite families over who have children around your child's age.

➤ Take your child and a friend or two shopping or out to lunch or inline skating—or do whatever appeals to them. Then, in gentle and encouraging ways, give your child occasional social feedback, "It would have been nice if you had said thank you when Trudy let you eat some of her French fries."

➤ Reward your child for trying to make connections. You can do this with stickers, stars, or pats on the back. It's also very encouraging for you to say things like, "I liked the way you offered Eric some of your candy. That's a nice way to show you want to be a friend" or "I'm glad you decided to join the other children playing so you could have fun, too."

➤ Support your child if he's having trouble making friends. This might include spending more time with him, listening to his complaints about other kids, or initiating activities with friends of the family or relatives.

➤ Sometimes instead of using praise, just notice your child's positive social behavior. You could say, "I saw how you let Mika play with your toys." Just your observation is a form of encouragement.

Sexual Matters

As noted earlier, sexual messages are everywhere. You'll never be able to keep your children from seeing billboards featuring a slinky female body, dressed in tight black satin, draping herself over a new car—or a tanned male body with his chest bare and his jeans partially unbuttoned. Prime-time television leaves little to the imagination. Such ads and messages are provocative, enticing, and confusing for children. Young people are a vulnerable audience, easily convinced that not only should they buy the products advertised, but they should look *and* act like the actors, models, and stars beamed at them.

When we teach parenting classes about children's sexuality, we often ask parents the following questions:

- What did you learn about sex and sexuality from your parents?
- What did you learn about sex and sexuality from television, songs, magazines, or books?
- What did you learn about sex and sexuality from your friends and/or siblings?
- What did you learn about sex and sexuality in school?

Our point is that most children are constantly learning about sexuality from a variety of sources. Often when we ask these questions, parents say, "I didn't learn anything about sex from my parents, they never talked about it." Our response to this statement is usually something like, "Well, it sounds like you *did* learn something; you learned you weren't supposed to talk about sex with your parents!"

A big key to helping your child with sexual development is to become what's been called "an askable parent." This means you should act in ways so your child believes he can ask you questions about sex. It also means you need to prepare for your child's questions about sex because you never know when he'll ask: "Hey, Mom, did you and dad have to have sex to have me?"

If you respond to your child's sex questions by turning beat red and dashing out of the room, you'll be teaching him that sex and sexuality are uncomfortable topics. But he'll still be curious and may then turn to other sources for sexual information. That leads us to another good reason to be an askable parent: Would you rather your child learn about sexual stuff from you or from the television or from his friends when he's riding home from school on the bus?

Instead of reacting with embarrassment or anxiety, we recommend that you almost always respond to your child's sex questions with a statement like, "Well, that's a great question, I'm glad you asked me." Then, depending on whether you feel prepared to discuss it or not, you can defer ("That's such a good question I'm going to think hard about my answer and talk with you later") or get into a discussion right on the spot.

We're not advocates of massive censorship, but we do think children should be protected from too much sexual or violent entertainment. More importantly, you should, at least occasionally, watch television with your child—even if it's only to check out what they are watching these days. And you should talk to him about sexuality, whenever the opportunity arises (and it arises often). Also, be sure to talk about the unreality of media sexual messages, and dangers of believing all that stuff.

Considering Your Child's Age and Temperament

All children go through developmental phases, at their own individual pace, during which they're quite interested in differences between males and females, where babies come from, and other aspects of human sexuality. They're also likely to go through phases during which they could hardly care less. Boys quite commonly go through a phase that involves trying on mom's or sister's clothes or makeup, and girls will sometimes insist on dressing in jeans and T-shirts for years. Most children will go through times of having only same-sex playmates and other times of having opposite-sex playmates. This is true both for children who eventually develop into heterosexual adults and those who develop into homosexual or bisexual adults.

Even very young children experience sexual feelings, and their body parts register pleasurable sensations. For example, consider the following story shared by a parent in a parenting class on preschoolers and sexuality:

My three-year-old daughter Emily really loves riding in the car in her car seat. I didn't realize it at first, but several weeks ago I noticed her making a bunch of pleasure sounds as we drove around and suddenly I figured out that she wiggles sort of, uh, well, she moves back and forth in her seat and she stimulates herself. I realized she's masturbating in her car seat. Then, and this is the worst part, my mom and I were driving around and Emily was in her seat in the back and she started making her happy and pleasure sounds and my mom sort of turned around and then said, "Well, she sure seems to like riding around in that seat." And I said, "Oh yeah, she does." We just sat there in dead silence for a minute. I had no idea what to say because even though I'm thirty years old, my mother and I have never been able to talk about sexual stuff.

+27++3+2+

It's not unusual for preschool-age children to be very interested in their sexual body parts—as well as being interested in other people's sexual body parts. And, as illustrated in the preceding story, many children embarrass their parents with their bold exploration of positive sexual sensations.

Interestingly, from ages five or six until puberty, your child's sexual interests may, quite normally, subside or become dormant. Or, depending on his temperament, he may be very modest. Or, he may like to "escape" from his clothes and run around the house naked at every opportunity. With all these possible variations in the way he might develop, how can you know when there's a sexual problem?

Troubling Behaviors and Recommended Responses

Okay, here's where we start talking about the sexual stuff that most parents consider very uncomfortable. Are you ready?

Touching to Explore

We'll talk first about masturbation. If your child masturbates or touches his private parts in public, you may find this upsetting. If it happens, you have several choices:

- You can immediately respond out of your own embarrassment and scold or shame your child.
- You can ignore the behavior and hope it goes away.
- You can gently remind your child that private parts are private and should not be touched in public places.

We support the last of these three options, the gentler one. We strongly believe this is the best choice—even if you think masturbation is morally wrong or offensive.

Here's why.

If you respond to your child's touching himself with shock, shouting, and embarrassment, you're drawing significant attention to a normal behavior that sometimes interests all children. Your strong reaction may scare your child. He may think, "It feels good to touch myself, but my mom and dad get so upset, it must really be very bad." Then, at some point, if your child becomes confused about his sexuality, he'll probably remember your extremely strong reaction and be too scared to talk to you about his confusion. Instead, if he's lucky, he'll find someone else who can talk openly and calmly about sexual matters without causing him to feel fear or shame. Or he may simply take his sexual feelings underground, choosing to never talk with anyone about them. Even worse, parental overreactions or rigid, one-sided morality lectures can sometimes make the activity even more interesting to your child.

Your best bet is to focus on helping your child understand and respect his body and the bodies of others, but not to make him feel ashamed. Also, stay calm, frank, and honest so your child isn't tempted to behave in sexual ways just because it's fun to get you all tied in knots.

When Children Play Doctor

It's not uncommon among siblings, cousins, or friends of a similar age to explore each other's bodies. Viewing and touching each other's naked or partially naked bodies can be, from the children's perspectives, both exciting and educational—but as we all know, it can easily become very damaging as well. While mild, mutually agreed-upon, showing of body parts is just another of many childhood events, any interactions that involve force or coercion are likely to do harm. Therefore, if your child plays "doctor" with another child, take these steps:

- Have another one of those honest, but non-scolding discussions about unacceptable touching.

- Evaluate whether or not there was any force or coercion involved—and if one of the children is much larger, much smarter, or much older than the other—enlist a professional to help with evaluation and possible counseling.

- Keep a closer eye on your child when he's playing with other children.

Unfortunately, your child may be touched sexually by another child or an adult who's older or bigger and stronger. That's one of the reasons he needs you to provide regular sexual education and discussions about good touch and bad touch. These discussions will help your child protect himself.

Your child probably has few words to communicate his discomfort or distress about sexual issues. Therefore, you need to be on the alert for signals that your child's sexual development isn't going well. Review the following checklist for clues about whether your child may be having a serious problem in this area.

Signs of a Serious Problem with Sexual Development

❑ My child has shown a sudden change from dressing like the other kids to dressing quite provocatively, asking to wear makeup, and is wanting to hang out with much older, or streetwise, children.

❑ My child is masturbating on a daily basis and in public situations.

❑ My child often tries to touch or comment on others' private parts.

❑ My child has suddenly changed his language for sexual parts and sexual behaviors, using explicit sexual street language.

❑ My child regularly tries to sneak peeks at other family members or guests when they're dressing or bathing.

❑ My child is extremely shy or inhibited about his body. This shyness has emerged quickly and is a big change from past behavior and this change is not associated with the onset or coming of puberty.

If your child engages in any of the behaviors on this checklist, at the very least, he needs caring, open conversations with you or another adult close to him. There are reading materials and classes available for children and parents that can help as starting points for these conversations. If conversations, along with guidance and education, don't seem to make a difference in your child's behaviors, then it's probably time to consult with a mental health professional.

When Sexual Behavior Is Forced

Some children, more commonly boys than girls, exhibit *predatory behavior*—even at young ages. The term "predatory" refers to behaviors intended to dominate, intimidate, humiliate, or otherwise bring someone under the predator's control. Bullying is an example of predatory behavior, and some predatory behaviors are sexual—when the predator seeks sexual gratification from an unwilling victim. Children who make fun of, bother, or intimidate others do so for many reasons, but it's not healthy for older, stronger children to impose their wishes on smaller children. Children need help in understanding how to behave in respectful ways with other, perhaps physically weaker, children. This is a special challenge for parents, as bullying and other predatory behaviors are often modeled in movies and television shows. Society still has far too many examples of men treating women with disrespect and not only getting away with it, but being seen as strong or admirable because of it.

Sexual predatory behavior is especially troubling. Predatory sexual behaviors include forcing or convincing another child to undress, be fondled, or fondle the predator, look at pornography, or engage in other sexual interactions. If your child engages in sexual predatory behavior even once, you should begin to watch your child closely while, at the same time, pursuing social and sexual education, and possibly therapy.

If your child is sexually victimized, even mildly, use the experience to improve communication and to further protect your child. Children can get over such unfortunate and damaging sexual experiences, but these experiences should not be taken lightly. Let your child know that what happened doesn't make him a bad person, nor does it change his sexual development. Also let him know it isn't his fault that it happened. Helping your child learn assertiveness skills, giving him guidance on how to figure out if a situation is potentially dangerous, and talking with him about self-care are all important, even more so if he has been victimized.

Unwanted sexual experiences can be very traumatic for your child. In Chapter 7, we talk about reactions to stressful events in life. Read Chapter 7 for further information if you suspect your child has endured a sexual trauma.

More Ways You Can Help Your Child

Talking about sexual matters with children isn't easy for most parents. But even if you've avoided talking with your children about sexual issues, you play a central role in your child's sexual beliefs and knowledge, and to a lesser degree, in his behaviors. As mentioned earlier, even if you choose *not* to talk with your child about sex, you're teaching an important and powerful message about sexuality. The "Helpful Hints" on page 112 can help make it easier to talk with your child about sex if you decide to do so.

Helpful Hints for Your Child's Sexual Problems

➤ Talk. Yes, *talk.* Use correct anatomical terms, like vagina, breast, and penis, although, in addition, you can also use terms that help your child communicate. Early on, tell your child that some body parts are private and special. Be careful that your own shyness doesn't give the all too common alternative message— that parts of our bodies are private and *shameful.*

➤ If children masturbate in public, assure them this activity is normal, but should be done in private.

➤ Don't allow your children to view pornographic materials. Especially watch out for the Internet.

➤ Discuss the sexual messages in the media, and contrast these messages with your own views and family values. Rather than having the "official" talk about the birds and the bees all at once, have these talks regularly, when the opportunity presents itself.

➤ Become an accurate source of information verbally, but don't push more information than your child's ready for.

➤ Have books available, complete with pictures of bodies, so your children will have an accurate idea of what normal male and female bodies look like.

Getting Professional Help

There are three ways of behaving related to sexual development that show a possible need for professional help. Strongly consider taking your child for evaluation or counseling if he:

• *is unwilling or unable to stop acting out in sexual ways.* Examples include repeated public masturbation, bothering others sexually, repeated vulgar language, or way too much interest in sexual touch.

• *refuses to acknowledge his sex, or anything to do with sexual development.* For example, your son may claim he isn't really a boy. Or, he may be so painfully inhibited that he can't undress to change clothes for gym, or he shows clear preferences for all things related to the other sex. If, even after long talks, and patient waiting, this confusion continues, professional help is advisable.

- *has been forced into sexual activity by someone else.* Take your child to a hospital emergency room, which should have standard procedures for evaluating children who have been sexually abused or raped. Or, ask your child's pediatrician or school counselor where you can get help if your child has been sexually assaulted or exposed to pornographic sexual material.

In contrast to this last issue of sexual abuse, the first two on this list are sexual development issues, which are best handled by having a talk with a professional before you take your child for an evaluation or counseling. Otherwise, there's potential for doing further harm, or making things more difficult in this sensitive area of sexuality. Children have a hard enough time finding ways to talk about sexual development with people who know and love them. Before taking a child with sexuality problems to a professional, ask his school counselor, pediatrician, or a mental health professional for advice on how to prepare your child for an evaluation or counseling session.

Summing It Up

Learning to get along with others and express needs and attractions appropriately is an essential task of childhood. If your child is painfully shy, unable to engage in cooperative play with other children, or so extroverted that no one can get a word in edgewise, he most likely needs help in learning basic social skills. He can learn these skills in natural social settings, in groups, and in family counseling. If these options don't seem to help, then individual counseling might be necessary. Individual counseling might help you and your family better understand the social problems, and thereby provide tools to address them.

Sexual attitudes and preferences develop early. Your child may get enormously mixed and difficult messages about sex through the media, which often pairs sexual imagery with a wide range of unrelated products. Models used in advertising can give your child impossible messages about the ideal body and contradictory messages about appropriate sexual attitudes and behaviors. As a result, your child may end up acting out sexually in ways that are unacceptable to you or your community. He'll need group or individual help to learn and practice more appropriate sexuality.

Check It Out

Boy v. Girl? How Gender Shapes Who We Are, What We Want, and How We Get Along by George Abrahams and Sheila Ahlbrand (Minneapolis: Free Spirit Publishing, 2002). We recommend this book for help with gender role discussions.

Dreamworlds II produced by Sut Jhally (Northampton, MA: Media Education Foundation, 1995). For those interested in understanding the music television messages delivered to our children, we strongly recommend this powerful video. It graphically shows the sexual messages children are getting in music videos, as well as elsewhere. You may wish to view it with older children, but we highly recommend that first you view it alone or with other parents. It contains graphic, condensed material that can be quite disturbing.

The Friendship Factor: Helping Our Children Navigate Their Social World by Kenneth H. Rubin (New York: Viking, 2002). "The friendship factor" is a missing piece to what really matters for a child's healthy emotional development. This book shows that the ability to connect socially is something children learn and can develop over time.

How to Talk with Teens About Love, Relationships, and S-E-X by Amy G. Miron and Charles D. Miron (Minneapolis: Free Spirit Publishing, 2001). This is a valuable guide for those all-important talks with teens.

Ten Talks Parents Must Have with Their Children About Sex and Character by Pepper Schwartz and Dominic Cappello (New York: Hyperion Press, 2000). This book also offers excellent guidance for talking with teens.

Where Did I Come From? by Peter Mayle, illustrated by Arthur Robins (Secaucus, NJ: Carol Publishing Group, 1993). We really like this entertaining, approachable book. It's informative, funny, and straightforward, and can help you talk with your younger child about sex.

You can also check out the resources listed at the end of Chapter 3 (pages 62–63). Gender and sexual development are obviously closely related to our bodies, the messages we get about them, and how we adjust to their changes.

Chapter 7

When Tough Things Happen to Nice Kids: Stress and Trauma

Matthias turned his face to the wall bereft of any tears or lamentation after the stresses of the experience he had recently come through. The death of his old and valued friend left a feeling like a large leaden lump inside his chest. He curled up and tried to hide within himself.

—**Brian Jacques,** *Redwall*

Life can seem grossly unfair, especially for children. Despite your best intentions, your child cannot be protected from all the stresses, traumas, or injustices of life. Everyone realizes that no one gets to live the perfect life, free from disappointment, pain, loss, and trauma, but we adults who care about children often wish we could protect them from the cold, cruel realities of the world. Nevertheless, divorces occur, parents die, school shootings happen—even terrorism and other national and global tragedies can disrupt children's lives.

If your child is exposed to stress, trauma, and tragedy, the key questions are practical ones: How much stress, trauma, or tragedy is too much for your child to handle? What are the signs that she needs extra help coping with a tough life situation or tragic turn of events? What can you do to help your child cope with the painful realities of life?

Nine-year-old Jennifer's parents separated after several years of marital difficulty. Both parents wanted to keep the children away from their disagreements, but doing so was very hard. Occasionally, Jennifer was exposed to her parents' arguing, yelling, door slamming, and cold, hard silence. After the divorce, Jennifer and her younger brother, Jimmy, went back and forth to each parent's house on a regular basis. Jimmy didn't seem to mind, or even really notice, but it was another story with Jennifer. She begged her parents to get back together, cried herself to sleep at least twice a week, became fearful of going to school, complained of nausea and headaches, and even began occasionally wetting the bed. Both parents grew increasingly concerned. Jennifer wasn't doing schoolwork, wasn't eating well, and even after three months, was still very emotionally upset by her parents' separation and upcoming divorce.

≈≈≈≈≈≈≈≈

After living his first 11 years in a small western city, close to his grandparents and other relatives, Jeremy's parents moved to a larger eastern city to pursue a new job opportunity. The family income increased substantially, with the family now occupying a larger house in an upper middle-class neighborhood, complete with a swimming pool. Though never an easygoing child, Jeremy became increasingly defiant and angry. Other children in the neighborhood initially sought Jeremy out, but stopped approaching him after he repeatedly "blew his top" when they refused to play the games he wanted to play.

Jeremy's parents tried reasoning with him about the advantages of their new home and neighborhood, but he insisted that, more than anything, he just wanted to move back home. Months after the move, he still became visibly sad, and then angry, following every phone conversation with his grandparents. His parents kept hoping that Jeremy would grow comfortable with his new home over time, but it seemed to them that things were getting worse, despite their efforts to help him adjust.

≈≈≈≈≈≈≈≈

When she was nine years old, Hannah's family home in Florida was destroyed by a major hurricane. The family lost everything, including two beloved pets and extensive family memorabilia. Her father suffered numerous serious injuries as the result of flying debris. He was in the hospital for several weeks, and it was more than six months before he returned to work. In the meantime, the family lived in a series of temporary settings; they lived with relatives, in a hotel, and in a rental trailer. It took more than 18 months for Hannah's family to build a new home in another location and move in. In the wake of the disaster, Hannah changed from a bright, happy child to a frightened, withdrawn child. She played alone, often reenacting themes of damage, loss, and injury; and she often woke screaming from frightening nightmares. Even after many months passed, she had difficulty falling asleep and staying asleep. In addition to her fearfulness, she began having angry outbursts toward family members that were terribly disproportionate to the situation.

The family moved into the new house, hoping Hannah would finally return to her happy and well-adjusted self, but she still insisted on playing alone, still had nightmares, and still refused to go outside if the weather was the least bit stormy. Though her parents believed their lives had stabilized, Hannah still seemed caught in the storm, unable to put it behind her.

All these children experienced stressful life events. The stressful events in Jennifer's and Jeremy's lives weren't unusual, in that many young people have divorced parents or are forced to move away from family and friends. Hannah's experiences, however, were more traumatic and unusual. In each scenario, the children's stress reactions deserve attention.

Troubles with Stress

It's possible for your child to have a wide assortment of reactions to stress. But, before we explore how stress can cause troubles for your child, first let's look at how stress is defined.

What Is Stress?

Mental health professionals define stress as *a challenge to our physical or psychological well-being requiring adjustment.* Positive events, such as receiving a school award, and negative events, such as getting a detention, both can be stressful for your child. Rapid, shallow breathing, increased heart rate and blood pressure, upset stomach or "butterflies," headaches, and heart palpitations are common physical reactions to stressful events. Additionally, your child's emotions and behaviors can be affected; when stressed, children feel scared, sad, grumpy, or even mad. In more severe cases, when the stressful event is perceived as life-threatening, your child may react by reliving the stressful event repeatedly; suffering sleep difficulties, including nightmares; avoiding circumstances or people associated with the event; and being easily startled.

Of course, there's nothing wrong with your child if she has a strong emotional or physical reaction to a scary, threatening, or stressful situation. When your child is threatened with danger, becoming sad, anxious, irritable, or having physical symptoms is expected and normal. In fact, there may be more cause for concern if your child doesn't look and act distressed in the face of stress. You're not getting any clues about what's going on—on the inside. So if your child has an obvious emotional reaction to a scary accident, a death in the family, or some other difficult situation, the good news is this: at least she hasn't pushed her feelings underground. Overall, your child's reactions to stress aren't a major problem unless they're out of proportion to the situation, go on too long, or are so extreme that they're threatening to her health or safety.

Stress Reactions, Big and Small

The ways children respond to external stressful events vary tremendously. This is partly because the effects of stress are made worse or better by how a child thinks about the event. If your child believes that an event is terrible, horrible, and out of her control, her stress response will be greater. However, if she finds a way to control or manage a stressful situation, her overall stress experience will be far less. An inspiring book that illustrates this fact about people is *Man's Search for Meaning* by Viktor E. Frankl (see "Check It Out" on page 130). Dr. Frankl survived being held prisoner in a concentration camp in Nazi Germany. Of course, we hope your child will never face anything even close to that kind of horrific stress, but Dr. Frankl's ability to find meaning and personal control in the midst of a concentration camp situation illustrates the power of human thinking over enormous stress.

There are other factors, in addition to how children think about trauma and stress, that make their stress reactions bigger or smaller. For example, your child's general physical health and disposition will affect how she handles stress. If she's in good health, she'll probably stand up to stress better. Past experiences with stress can also be important. If your child handled mild stress successfully before, then she might manage larger amounts of stress well in the future. On the other hand, many stresses can pile up and have a rather nasty cumulative effect. Getting behind in school may stress your child, but facing a big exam the day after she sprained her ankle and a week after her mom delivered a baby brother can take a major toll on not only her exam performance, but also on her physical health. In fact, research has shown that people who experience very large or repeated stressful events are more prone to physical illness and accidents.

Your child's belief in her ability to succeed at something will also influence how well she copes with stress. For example, imagine two girls preparing to take a math test. One feels proficient in math, has studied for the test, and feels confident from the minute she walks into the room. When the test is handed out, this girl is a little nervous at first, but soon sees that the questions are manageable, so her stress level quickly drops. The second girl, who is less prepared and has less math aptitude—or less belief in her math aptitude, feels very tense right from the start. Through the course of the exam, the first child feels less and less anxiety as she works on it; the second child gets more and more anxious, and these growing emotional reactions make it very difficult for her to complete the test successfully.

Later in this chapter, we'll talk about the big unusual traumas outside the realm of daily life stressors. Of course, it's impossible to create one distinct category for *normal* disappointments, upsets, and losses, and one for *worse than normal,* because as mentioned earlier, everyone reacts to stress differently. However, in general terms, life has predictable sad, scary, or disappointing events that all or most of us face. These include the deaths of loved ones; performance failures or disappointments in school, athletics, music, or other areas of personal importance; fender benders; being bullied by someone; broken bones; ongoing conflicts with friends; divorces; and getting lost at the mall or on a hike.

Considering Your Child's Age and Temperament

Probably from birth, children notice when they lose something important to them, and respond with grief or protest. However, the expression of grief, or the handling of stressful life events, depends on your child's developmental level. Especially in the areas of stress and loss, we need to remember that children are *not* adults, and they don't think like adults. For instance, your child's sense of time, her understanding of how big things are, and her beliefs about her control over the world vary markedly with her age. Therefore, when stress or trauma occurs, your child will be affected quite differently than another child experiencing the same stress or loss at a different age.

Temperament, too, plays a big role in handling stress and loss. Some children need lots of physical contact and lots of talk time when dealing with grief or stress. Others tend to withdraw into themselves and need to draw, write things, and mull. Children with calm, optimistic temperaments might absorb certain stresses more easily than children with more irritable or anxious temperaments.

When your child is faced with normal stresses, she'll probably have a normal stress reaction. She'll feel frightened, upset, angry, or sad. She'll need time to grieve, talk, think, pout, cry, or whatever else she needs to do to work things through. She'll also need comfort from you and opportunities to talk and play with her most trusted family members and friends.

Research on stress and health and mental health is very clear: Without some form of self-expression, stressful experiences accumulate and result in adverse effects. Therefore, if your child has been exposed to stress, the first and best thing to do is to help her express her thoughts and feelings about the stressful event. Unfortunately, as you probably know, children are notorious for *not* talking or *not* wanting to talk with their parents—or sometimes anyone—about what's bothering them. In the opening example at the start of this chapter, although Jennifer clearly needs to talk with someone about her parents' divorce, she simply refuses to, choosing instead to limp along in emotional and psychological pain.

The Usual Diagnosis

When a child is struggling with a stressful life event, and the struggle isn't going well, mental health professionals label this as *adjustment disorder*. This label may apply if your child has significant emotional or behavioral problems related to a stressful life event (or events)—including events that happened as much as three months before. These problems might show up in school, at home, or in social relationships.

One piece of good news is that if your child is diagnosed with an adjustment disorder, most insurance policies will pay for counseling from a licensed mental health provider. Some parents are surprised by the fact that medical insurance pays for personal problems associated with a normal stressful event. However, we think it makes perfect sense. Stressful events can make a wide range of health problems much worse. For example, after experiencing stress, children are more likely to suffer from colds, flu, or other normal childhood ailments. Additionally, if children have existing health problems such as asthma or diabetes, untreated stress can make the conditions worse. Finally, if emotional and psychological stress is completely unaddressed, children are more likely to later suffer from more severe emotional or behavioral problems such as depression, anxiety, eating disorders, or substance abuse.

Signs of a Serious Problem with Stress

❑ My child reacts to a stressful situation in a way that's out of character for her.

❑ My child's reaction to stress is causing lots of family turmoil.

❑ My child's grades are dropping because of her strong reaction to stress. Her teachers are complaining about her behaving in unusual ways.

❑ My child has suddenly become so irritable that it seems she's fighting everyone.

❑ My child is suddenly getting involved in far more social activities than seems healthy.

❑ My child's teachers and I have tried normal consoling and comforting that usually have worked in the past but now don't seem to be helping.

❑ My child has had a number of chances to work through her stressful reaction—for more than a month—and yet she is still having an unusually strong emotional reaction.

As you sort through the "Signs of a Serious Problem with Stress" list, here's something important to consider: Most of us make it through difficult times without counseling. However, counseling, support groups, and other types of professional help can shorten the struggle, making things get better faster. In addition, researchers have proven that counseling also serves to build stronger, more resilient coping styles, so that next time, stress won't take the same toll. As one stress researcher has said, we need to teach our children how to practice "safe stress."

Getting Professional Help

Support groups made up of children with similar struggles are often a great source of help for children as young as four years old. Whether the issue is divorce, loss of a loved one, or a more severe tragedy, such as witnessing a murder, being in a group with other children who've had similar stressful events in their lives can be very healing. Grief groups can be enormously helpful as soon as two or three months after a death, and continue to be a helpful experience, even years after a loss. Children give positive ratings to divorce support groups both during and after a divorce.

Depending upon where you live, there may be many different kinds of support groups available to your child. Usually, you can find out about these different support groups either by reading about them in your local newspaper, by calling an information helpline, or by contacting your local city-county health department. Also, schools and school counselors are excellent sources of information about support groups for children.

A friend of ours who directs a bereavement camp, an outdoor summer camp for children who have had a parent or sibling die, shared the following story:

One night, after all the camp activities ended, there were about 20 campers and staff hanging around the fire in the lodge area. In particular, three young boys had each paired up with one of our male staff members. All three of these boys had lost their dads within the past two years. One of the boys had wiggled his way into his camp counselor's arms and was crying. It wasn't just a few tears leaking out; he was sobbing, his chest heaving and tears flowing. What was best about this situation was that this young boy was able to express the pain of losing his father, right in front of 19 other children—and everyone there had some sense of what he was feeling. After about an hour, the camp counselor carried the youngster to his bed, comforting him along the way.

Unfortunately, bereavement is a common childhood occurrence. There are many helpful books for you to read with your child (see page 131), and you may find good programs such as our friend's bereavement camp in your community. Most communities have local hospice services to assist dying people and their families, and they can provide you with information about local bereavement resources as well.

As in this camp experience, if your daughter meets and talks with other children who are experiencing similar disappointments or stresses, she'll probably feel great relief. She'll realize she's not alone; others have lost loved ones or had families break up. She'll hear others talk about similar sad or angry feelings. She'll listen to, and talk about, coping strategies and begin to believe life will go on and that she'll be okay.

Children often initially resist going to support groups, but usually warm up after a couple meetings and will value the experience. So, if there's a group available that has a decent reputation, take advantage of it. Such groups are both *interventive*, addressing symptoms and troubles in the child at the present time, and *preventive*, teaching the child new ways to think and new coping mechanisms that might keep things from getting worse at a later time.

Unlike with group support, children who go for individual counseling may tend to think of themselves as "the problem." Children of divorce, bullied children, or children who've lost loved ones are all likely to think that the bad things that happened to them are their fault. They're likely to think they're inadequate, bad, and that somehow, they brought this on themselves or their families. Being taken to counseling, if not handled well, can confirm your child's worst fears: "Yes, indeed, Keesha, you're the problem here. The rest of us are fine, but *you* need help."

When possible, instead of taking your child to therapy to deal with *her* problem, consider family therapy, even if you have only one child who's struggling. Of course, don't be surprised if your family, or particular family members, resist. Generally, no one really likes the idea of needing to go to an expert for emotional or "mental" help. On the other hand, as a parent, be willing to go to therapy with your child, if only to communicate the healthy message: "We're in this together as a family and so we'll all be going for a brief family emotional tune-up."

In divorce situations, cooperative whole-family therapy work is unlikely. However, it's possible to have one parent go along one time, and the other the next, to give your child the message that she hasn't lost either parent's love or care and that the parents, although separated, are joined when it comes to providing emotional support.

If your family is going through a separation or divorce, we strongly recommend that you attend a parenting class for divorcing parents. Many states, counties, and provinces require that divorced and never married parents take these classes, for good reason. As it turns out, about 75 percent of parents—even parents who are forced by the courts to take these classes—say they're glad they did. This is because, after a divorce, parents and children are both facing a new and challenging situation. Also, as a parent, you may still be in conflict with your child's mom or dad and divorce classes can help you move beyond your resentments and toward a more constructive focus on your children.

A Bill of Rights for Children of Divorce

By John and Rita Sommers-Flanagan

I am a child of divorce. I hold these truths to be self-evident:

I have the right to be free from your conflicts and hostilities. When you badmouth each other in front of me, it tears me apart inside. Don't put me in the middle or play me against my other parent. And don't burden me with your relationship problems, they're yours, not mine.

I have the right to develop a relationship with both my parents. I love you both. I know you'll sometimes be jealous about that, but you need to deal with it because you're the adult and I'm the child.

I have a right to information about things that will affect my life. If you're planning to divorce, I have a right to know, just as soon as is reasonable. Likewise, if you're planning to move, get remarried, or any other major life change, I have a right to know about it.

Just as I have a right to basic information about my life, I also have a right to be protected from bad information. This means you shouldn't tell me about sexual exploits or other misbehavior by my other parent. And don't apologize to me—for my other parent—because this implies a negative judgment of my other parent. If you apologize to me, apologize for yourself.

I have a right to my own personal space in both my homes. This doesn't mean I can't share a room with my brother or sister, but it does mean that I need you to give me some space and time of my own. I also need some special personal items in my own space. And this might include a picture of my other parent. Don't freak out about it.

I have a right to physical safety and supervision. I know you may be very upset about your divorce, but that doesn't mean you should neglect my needs. I don't want to be home alone all the time, while you're out dating some new person.

I have a right to spend time with both parents, without interference. My right to spend time with each of you shouldn't depend on how much money one of you has paid the other. That makes me feel cheap, like something you might buy in a store.

I have a right to financial and emotional support from both my parents, regardless of how much time I spend with either one of you. This doesn't mean I expect twice as much as other kids get, it just means you should stop worrying about what I got from my other parent and focus on what you're providing me.

I have a right to firm limits and boundaries and reasonable expectations. Just because I'm a child of divorce, doesn't mean I can't handle chores, homework, or other normal responsibilities. On the other hand, keep in mind that even though I may have a little sister or brother (or stepsister or stepbrother), I'm not the designated baby-sitter.

I have a right to your patience. I didn't choose to go through a divorce. I didn't choose to have my biological parents live in two different homes, move away, date different people, and in general, turn my world upside down. More than most children, my life has been beyond my control. This means I'll need your help and support to work through my control issues.

Finally, I have a right to be a child. I shouldn't have to be your spy, your special confidant, or your mother. Just because you hate to talk to each other, I shouldn't have to be your personal message courier. I exist because you created me. Therefore, I have a right to be more than a child of divorce. I have the right to be a child whose parents love me more than they've come to hate each other.

Helpful Hints for Your Child's Stress

➤ If you're feeling stress or trauma from the same event that affected your child, be sure to take time to care for yourself. When your child is safe and with another trusted person, consider the following activities:

- *Talk with someone about your stress. Express both your thoughts and your feelings.*

- *Start a journal and write about your experiences.*

- *Find a vigorous exercise routine that helps you cope with stress and practice that routine, over and over again, as needed.*

- *Meditate, use relaxation or imagery techniques, spend time in the hot tub, or find another healthy method for achieving calmness.*

➤ If your child is older or very mature, encourage her to use the preceding list of stress management strategies herself. It works best if you model these practices for her—and also do one of the following:

- *Schedule time to talk together.*

- *Slip in some talk-time when engaging in a mutually enjoyable activity.*

➤ If your child is younger or less verbal, the following strategies may be more effective than trying to get her to talk about whatever is bothering her.

- *Get out art supplies and have her do some drawing, painting, or sculpting of whatever's troubling her.*

- *Read her some supportive or therapeutic stories.*

- *Get on the floor and engage in some "pretend" play with her.*

Severe Trauma: Experiences Outside of the Normal Realm

The horrible truth is that children are vulnerable to potentially traumatic events every day, in many ways. As psychologists, we've worked with children who've witnessed murders, survived severe car wrecks, experienced physical or sexual abuse, were present at the accidental death of a friend, and were severely injured in fires or accidents.

As a parent, you're probably naturally aware of the fact that children can be emotionally scarred by traumatic events. Mental health professionals have named two major types of emotional responses to trauma—*posttraumatic stress disorder* and *acute stress disorder*, which are quite serious. These conditions are described more fully in the following sections. Of course, it's less important for you to know the names of these problems than to recognize the signs of severe stress or traumatic disturbance in your child.

Traumatic Stress Disorders

If your child has had the misfortune of witnessing, or being involved in, a horrible crime incident, or experiences some other extremely scary event such as a serious car accident or natural disaster, she may have become so overwhelmed she can't handle her everyday life. If this is the case, it's very likely that eventually she'll be diagnosed with *posttraumatic stress disorder* or PTSD. Common signs or symptoms of PTSD are listed below.

Signs of a Serious Problem with Trauma Reactions

❑ My child persistently reexperiences or relives the trauma through recurrent thoughts, repetitive play, or distressing dreams (nightmares). Also my child feels as if the traumatic event is recurring in her daily life. She flinches sometimes, as if she expects the bad thing to happen again.

❑ My child becomes distressed if anything happens that reminds her of the traumatic event.

❑ My child actively avoids situations that might, in any way, remind her of the trauma. She has become rather numb and responds very little to people, emotions, and life in general. My traumatized child might also be unable to recall important parts of the traumatic event.

❑ My child is more physically aroused or alert than normal since the traumatic event. She has difficulties with falling or staying asleep, is extra irritable, has unusual angry outbursts, can't seem to concentrate, is overly watchful or vigilant, or startles easily.

If your child has been exposed to a severe trauma and has any of the symptoms on the preceding list, seeking professional help is an excellent idea.

Your child could also have a slightly different and more sudden or acute reaction to trauma, instead of the more drawn-out symptoms on the checklist. If, for example, immediately after your child was caught in a life-threatening robbery situation, she said she felt numb, was emotionally unresponsive, appeared to be in a daze, and talked like the whole traumatic experience was unreal, she might be having a traumatic reaction called *acute stress disorder*. After being caught in a trauma, some children we've worked with have told us things like, "I thought I was watching a movie!" And "sometimes I'm still not sure it really happened."

It's very important for you to remember that there's nothing wrong or weak or sick or disturbed about your child if she reacts with trauma symptoms after she's been exposed to a terrible event. It's normal to experience some if not all of the symptoms, and most children (and adults) benefit from professional help and support following a traumatic experience.

In one of the examples at the beginning of the chapter, Hannah's exposure to the hurricane that destroyed her home, killed her pets, and injured her father was very traumatic for her. One way she tried to work through the trauma was reenacting the events through play. This is a very common strategy children use. Because they aren't as verbal as adults, they use play to tell the awful story over and over, and in this way, to possibly achieve mastery over it.

Following a trauma, your child may have nightmares, find it harder to concentrate, and act immature for her age. For instance, a child who outgrew thumb-sucking may start up again. Or a child who had become happily independent might be clingy. Bed-wetting is not uncommon, and favorite teddy bears, blankets, or pillows that had been discarded may become very important again. Children are likely to avoid anything that might remind them of the trauma (except when reenacting the trauma through play), and may experience flashbacks of the event.

Getting Professional Help

If your child has experienced a trauma, there are many ways you can help with healing. First, recognize that emotional trauma doesn't end just as soon as the event is over. If your child went through, or witnessed, a traumatic event, it's likely that you'll benefit from professional consultation and that your child will benefit from counseling or some other form of intervention.

A support group can be very helpful for your child shortly after experiencing a traumatic event. In some cases where many people go through the same traumatizing experience, there will be an immediate chance for your child to participate in a procedure that's called a "stress debriefing." Usually, everyone who was exposed to the traumatizing stress is eligible to participate (depending on the criteria of the organization that sponsors it) and so you may be contacted about it by the sponsoring organization. Or, you can find out about the groups in your newspaper or other media outlet. If your child is eligible and you want her to participate, she will be grouped together with other children and adults who have experienced the stress and they'll all get to talk about the trauma together. We recommend that you have your child take advantage of this debriefing opportunity, because doing so can reduce later stress-related problems. Also, schools or community agencies often offer support groups for children who have PTSD.

At some point after your child is traumatized, you may decide to take her to counseling. If so, be sure to look for a counselor who's experienced in working with children who've been exposed to trauma. Keep in mind that several different approaches to helping children with trauma reactions are available. Depending upon your child's age, these approaches will include some or all of the following techniques:

- *play therapy*—Your child gets a chance to work through her response to the trauma through playful activities.

- *relaxation*—Your child learns to relax her body and mind and let go of the tension and fear connected to the trauma.

- *practice*—Your child gets a chance to practice, either in reality or in her mind, facing the feared situations or people.

- *talking*—Your child gets to talk about her horrible experience and future fears with a safe, trusted adult.

Helpful Hints for Your Child's Traumatic Reactions

➤ Find a support group for your child.

➤ Make reasonable home safety accommodations that your child requests, including adding locks to the door, leaving lights on, bolting windows, and so on. Monitor television shows, and screen other media exposure for anything that might resemble the trauma.

➤ Be ready to talk any time your child seems open, but don't force conversations. Be a good listener. Don't allow anything you say to even remotely suggest your child was to blame for the trauma—even by her being in the wrong place at the wrong time.

➤ If you're able, share your own feelings with your child. Let her see your sensitive side, but at the same time, stay in control so you don't enhance her fears because you seem emotionally unstable.

➤ Outside of the family, choose carefully who you tell about the events, and do so for loving reasons. Let your child know which extended family members or friends know about the experience. Honor any requests for privacy your child may make.

➤ Be patient. Even if your child is in a good support group or seeing a counselor, working through trauma takes time. There may be periods when she'll withdraw and other times when she'll be irritable or extra alert. Eventually, if you provide a safe, caring, and loving environment, she'll become more peaceful and no longer feel so disturbed by what happened.

Summing It Up

Life can be stressful and traumatic for your child despite your best intentions. If your child has prolonged difficulties adjusting to an upsetting life event, mental health professionals refer to this as an adjustment disorder. In such cases, counseling can often help hasten the child's recovery and strengthen coping skills.

If your child is exposed to trauma—to events that are uncommon, threatening, or overwhelming, it's highly likely she'll benefit from group or individual counseling. You may find it helpful to get support and consultation as well. Exposure to trauma takes a large emotional toll on human beings. Traumatic experiences are neither easily dealt with nor easily forgotten. Therefore, children coping with trauma need a large dose of adult caring, compassion, and assistance.

Check It Out

Recommended Books on Stress and Trauma

Man's Search for Meaning by Viktor E. Frankl (New York: Washington Square Press, 1985). Frankl's classic describes his experiences in a Nazi concentration camp. The book illustrates the power of the mind and meaning over stress.

Trauma and Recovery by Judith Herman (New York: Basic Books, 1997). This book is a classic. It provides a general overview of the effects of trauma, and although it doesn't directly address children in particular, it offers a thorough foundation of knowledge about trauma.

Recommended Books on Grief

The Fall of Freddie the Leaf: A Story of Life for All Ages by Leo Buscaglia (New York: Henry Holt and Company, 2002). This simple story illustrates how leaves change with the season and eventually fall to the ground. It's a nice initial introduction to the concept of death.

Helping Children Cope with the Loss of a Loved One: A Guide for Grownups by William Kroen (Minneapolis: Free Spirit Publishing, 1996). This practical book will help you find the right words to use as you talk with your child about the death of a loved one.

What on Earth Do You Do When Someone Dies? by Trevor Romain (Minneapolis: Free Spirit Publishing, 1999). When someone dies, children wonder why, how, what's next, is it my fault, and what's a funeral. This book answers these questions in a friendly and direct tone.

When Someone Very Special Dies: Children Can Learn to Cope with Grief Workbook by Marge Heegaard (Minneapolis: Woodland Press, 1992). This is another simple book designed to help kids understand death and begin to express their feelings about death.

Recommended Books on Divorce

Don't Divorce Us: Kids' Advice to Divorcing Parents by Rita Sommers-Flanagan, Chelsea Elander, and John Sommers-Flanagan (Alexandria, VA: American Counseling Association, 2000). We wrote this book to help children find words for what they fear, what they hope, and what they need. It's a collection of essays and input from hundreds of people who were children of divorce. It's not a bad book for divorcing parents, either (if we do say so ourselves)!

For Better or for Worse: Divorce Reconsidered by E. Mavis Hetherington and John Kelly (New York: W. W. Norton, 2002). In this book, renowned divorce researchers and clinical psychologist Mavis Hetherington reports some fairly optimistic findings from her 20-year study with about 1,400 families who have experienced divorce.

Juggling Act: Handling Divorce Without Dropping the Ball: A Survival Kit for Parents and Kids by Roberta Beyer and Kent Winchester (Minneapolis: Free Spirit Publishing, 2001). Here's a kit with numerous practical features for both children and parents facing divorce.

Mom's House, Dad's House: Making Two Homes for Your Child by Isolina Ricci (New York: Fireside, 1997). This book is always our first recommendation for parents who are divorcing, because it provides such an excellent and balanced view of shared parenting.

Chapter 8

Button-Pushing & Button-Pushers: Problems with Resistance, Disobedience, and Anger

Oh red, angry paint
Oh paint that scowls.
Oh blood so red.
Oh hate. Oh mad. Oh fear.
Oh noisy fights and smeary red.
Oh hate. Oh blood. Oh tears.
—**Virginia M. Axline, *Dibs in Search of Self***

Mark Twain once quipped: "When angry, count to four; when very angry, swear." After working with thousands of parents and children in our clinical practice, we can say without a doubt that handling anger constructively is one of life's more complex challenges—for both parents and children. In fact, we've discovered that many parents who seek professional assistance for their children's problems with anger do so because they've been surprised by the power and intensity of their *own* anger. A good place to start if you want to help your child with his anger is to make sure you're dealing with your own constructively (not in the manner Twain suggests!). We believe dealing with your own anger gracefully is so important, we've included information on anger management for parents in the "Check It Out" section at the end of this chapter (see page 146).

For children, anger is a mysterious and powerful emotion. Sometimes, anger just seems to come over them. Other times, children get angry with parents or other adults because they've been treated unfairly—or think they have. Once children get angry it's not unusual for them to be unable or unwilling to deal with their anger in socially acceptable ways. They dig in their heels, they refuse help or guidance, and they blow their corks!

It's homework time at the Joneses. Eleven-year-old Cal has comfortably settled into playing video games when his mother comes into his room.

Mom: Cal, it's time to stop your video games and get on to your homework. You're supposed to stop at 7 and it's already 10 after.

Cal: (gives no response but continues to play the game, focusing intently)

Mom: (returning 10 minutes later) Calvin, why are you still playing the video game? I told you it's time to stop and get on with your homework. Now!

Cal: (angrily) I'm right in the middle of my game! I can do my homework later.

Mom: Calvin, listen to me. It's time to stop now and get your books out.

Cal: I'm almost finished. I'll do it in a little bit.

Mom: Do it now! You're 20 minutes late as it is.

Cal: (starts yelling and banging his fist on the desk) I'm *not* going to do it until I get to the next level! You're always yelling at me and making me do things. I can take care of myself. (keeps banging his fists)

Mom: If you don't stop now, I'm taking away your video game system.

Cal: (starts screaming, yelling, and begins knocking objects around in the room).

Mom: (in raised, angry voice) Stop it! I'm tired of your disobedience! You're always arguing with me about everything.

Cal: It's not my fault! You're always bossing me around about something. I hate you! (storms angrily out of the room, goes to his bedroom, slams the door, and continues to yell for about another 10 minutes before he becomes quiet. When his mother peaks into the room, she sees he's fallen asleep on his bed.)

Like many parents, you may find the preceding scene with Calvin and his mom all too familiar. Of course, this scene isn't limited to children who play video games. Similar parent-child exchanges are likely to play out in many different situations. However, before concluding your child has a problem with anger and defiance, consider the following reasons why he might be especially irritable:

- He's hungry.
- He's tired.
- He's in physical pain.
- He's in emotional pain.

If your child is regularly angry or defiant, your first best plan is to check on whether his hunger, fatigue, or physical or emotional pain are causing his irritability. Then, once you're confident his immediate physical and emotional needs are taken care of, you can begin exploring whether he has a genuine problem with anger and defiance.

There are two main common triggers for your child's angry and defiant behavior:

- You're asking or telling him to do something he doesn't want to do (like a chore or to go to bed).
- You're asking or telling him to stop doing something he enjoys doing (like video games, television, or playing with friends).

As you can see, these two triggers have one main thing in common: they both involve you trying to exercise authority or influence over your child.

With this background information in mind, let's look at how mental health professionals define angry and defiant behavior in children.

What Is Oppositional-Defiant Behavior?

The terms *oppositional* and *defiant* are used together by mental health professionals to describe the sorts of behaviors we've been discussing so far in this chapter. In particular, if your child's consistent reaction to adult authority is to yell, scream, argue, throw a temper tantrum, and blame you for his problems, then professionals might consider labeling your child as having an *oppositional-defiant disorder*. In this chapter, we'll use the simpler term *defiant* to describe the troublesome behaviors, except when we're specifically referring to the official psychiatric condition of oppositional-defiant disorder.

Boys, more than girls, tend to act defiantly, and parents very commonly bring their children to see mental health professionals because of the obnoxious and aggressive quality that often accompanies such behavior. Nearly every day, we receive at least one phone call from a distraught, sometimes angry, and often fed up parent who says, "My child just won't listen!" Or "He never does anything around here!"

When big conflicts occur, as in the case of Calvin and his mom, parents and children often blame one another for the problem. Here's what Calvin and his mom had to say about each other when we talked to them in private:

Mom: It doesn't matter how I approach him, he's just looking for a fight!

Cal: She's always bossing me around. It's do this, do that. And what really pisses me off is that she never even asks me nicely!

Both Calvin and his mom are making important points. In truth, usually parents and children are both contributing to big family conflicts. As we described in Chapter 1, some children are very independent-minded at birth and are more likely to argue with their parents as they grow up, while others are naturally more calm and cooperative. But it's unfair to lay all the blame for defiant behaviors on children and their temperament. After all, many parents are too hung up on trying to control their children or use poor skills and strategies when they ask their child to cooperate or set limits on their child's behavior.

As you read this chapter, be sure to take a close look at yourself. Are you approaching your child in a way that encourages cooperation, or are you ordering him around and pushing his buttons in ways that might be causing him to resist your desires (similar to Calvin's mother)? We'll come back to this point again later in this chapter, and we'll also take a closer look at what Calvin's mother might have done differently to increase the likelihood of his cooperation.

Does Your Child Have a Problem with Oppositional-Defiant Behavior?

As you may suspect, defying authority figures is so common in children that it's nearly impossible to tell if your child is really troubled in this area or just being a normal kid. Just think how everyone expects lots of adamant "no's" from a two-year-old. In fact, most of us would quickly start worrying if our child was always 100 percent agreeable with parent and teacher demands and decisions. We look for signs of independence and self-sufficiency. In some ways, this puts children in a double bind: We expect them to speak up for themselves, but want them to do so in a polite and socially appropriate manner. Further, parents tend to admire their child's independence sometimes (when it's directed toward others), but when it comes flying straight at them, they're often considerably less enthused.

It can be very hard to define the difference between normal and healthy independent behavior in your child and less normal, defiant behavior. The checklist that follows is used by mental health professionals to determine if your child has a diagnosable oppositional-defiant disorder. Use it as a general guideline to help you determine whether to seek professional assistance concerning your child's behaviors. As you review the list, keep in mind that your child has to be clearly showing four or more of the following behaviors for over six months to be considered as having an oppositional-defiant disorder. Particularly note whether your child's defiant behaviors are causing him lots of distress or really getting in the way of his ability to participate in normal, healthy childhood activities.

Signs of a Serious Problem with Defiance or Anger

❑   My child often loses his temper. Coping with his anger outbursts becomes a regular part of my day.

❑   My child often argues with adults. Most typically, he will take a stand opposed to an adult and then fight hard for his position, almost always refusing to compromise.

❑   My child often refuses to follow adult directions. If I suggest that he brush his teeth, he usually ignores or rejects what I say.

❑   My child often deliberately goes out of his way to annoy other people. He almost seems to enjoy the reaction he gets from bothering others.

❑   My child often blames other people for his behavior problems. Poor school performance is almost always "the teacher's fault" or my fault.

❑   My child is easily annoyed by others. It's as if he's ready for a fight and then quickly responds with anger and indignation.

❑   My child is often angry and resentful. His typical mood is not always angry, but that's definitely his predominate mood.

❏ My child often shows a wish for revenge. His usual perception is that others are intentionally against him and so he often wants to get them back.

If you read the checklist closely, you might wonder what is meant by the word *often*. While it can seem vague, a good way to gauge whether your child's problem behavior fits the *often* criteria is to observe how other children his age behave. If your child, as a rule, acts in one of the ways listed above much more frequently than other children, that would be considered *often*. If four of the above behaviors occur often, talking with a mental health professional can help determine if your child has an *oppositional-defiant disorder*.

Another common response to the checklist is, "Well, that sounds like a description of the typical 21st Century child." It may seem that labeling a child who acts in these ways with *oppositional-defiant disorder* is making normal childhood behavior into a sickness or *pathology*. This is a very important consideration and so we encourage you to talk with trusted friends, teachers, and others if you're consistently worried about whether your child's defiant behaviors are in the normal childhood range or not.

Your child's defiant behavior can be a big challenge, especially if he acts this way repeatedly at home but rarely does so at school or around the neighborhood. This pattern can make you feel crazy: "The teachers say he's an angel at school. Well, I can tell you this: he's an absolute demon when he's at home." If your child is showing severe misbehavior at home, but behaving fine at school, try not to immediately blame yourself or your child. Focus on how and why the *interactions* between you and your child are working poorly and what you both might do to improve the situation. Closely examine your approaches to your child and his reactions. You might discover any one of the following:

- You're spending lots of time arguing with your child. Spending time arguing, even though it's negative, can be very rewarding for your child and will therefore increase his defiant behavior.
- You're not spending much time—especially positive time—with your child. This might cause him to think time spent arguing might be better than no time spent together at all.

- You and your child aren't communicating or listening very well to each other. Even sitting down together and agreeing to try hard can help with this.

- You and your child are very similar. Perhaps both of you have bossy temperaments.

In addition to looking for the preceding patterns, you can also consult with teachers, friends, or others. Getting an outside opinion might shed some light on why your child is behaving so much differently in different environments. By exploring what underlies these differences, you may eventually discover some changes you can make in your approach to parenting your child.

Considering Your Child's Age and Temperament

Even if your preschooler is defiant, it's unlikely that he'll be labeled or diagnosed as oppositional-defiant, because some resistant behavior is fairly common among preschoolers. On the other hand, it's certainly possible that in preschool years your child's anger and disobedience can become so frequent and intense enough that it warrants professional attention. One young mother who came for a parenting consult on her five-year-old told the following story:

The other night I wanted my son to clean up his room before we started his bedtime ritual. So, I just told him, "It's time for you to go upstairs to your room and pick up a few of your toys." He just stood there at the bottom of the stairs with his hands on his hips and stuck out his chin and said, "NO!" So I repeated myself, "Samuel, you need to get upstairs and pick up some of your toys and I'll be there in a few minutes." At that point he started glaring at me. His eyes bugged out and his face was totally intense and he finally spoke, using a line from a Clint Eastwood movie, he said, "You wanna piece of me?"

Generally speaking, problems associated with your child's defiant behavior increase as he gets older and becomes more physically and intellectually able to win arguments. That's why it's wise to learn to deal with your child's defiance early on. Information on how to manage defiant behavior is included later in this chapter, and additional resources are listed in "Check It Out" (see page 146).

While not as common in girls, being defiant is not limited to the male chromosome. We worked with a young woman (we'll call her

Jane) who at age eleven was described by a teacher as the mouthiest child she'd ever known. Jane's parents were beside themselves. They brought her to counseling after her third detention in three days for defiance and rudeness. When her parents tried talking with her about the incidents, she insisted the teachers were to blame for failing to give clear directions, for expecting perfection, and in one case, for "being a real prick." She complained that the school counselor was "stupid and annoying," and asked her parents to allow her to homeschool. By the end of the conversation, the family was in turmoil. It was clear that Jane and her family needed help.

Defiant behaviors occur for many reasons. One reason is that many very successful adults in the popular media display defiance, stubbornness, and generally rebellious personalities. The media loves extremely strong personalities like the *aggressive* businessperson, the *defiant* politician, the *unstoppable* athlete, and the *outspoken* musician or artist. If you read the newspaper, watch television, or peruse a few magazines, you'll quickly come to the conclusion that it's not the meek who are presently inheriting the earth. At least according to the media, the folks who will end up inheriting the earth are all those big personalities who throw their weight around.

Although defiance problems usually surface during preschool years, we've had parents tell us they thought the problem started sometime before birth. For example, one frustrated mom exclaimed, "Even before he was born he showed the same pattern. When I was up and awake and going through my regular day, the baby in my womb was quiet as a mouse. But, as soon as I'd lay down and try to sleep, he'd start kicking like some famous soccer player!"

This mom is making an important point about how defiant youth are created. As you can see from her complaint about her boy's in-utero behavior, she was beginning to expect and brace herself for a battle with her son even before he was born. The fact is that it's impossible to completely control children's behavior—inside or outside the womb. Therefore, rather than assuming an adversarial attitude like this mom, parents are better off adopting an attitude of curiosity and acceptance toward their young children. As it turns out, when parents expect their children to be oppositional and defiant and then label them as "difficult," the children are much more likely to fulfill their parent's prophecy. The fulfillment of this prophecy may be less of a testament to the power of temperament and more of a testament to the influence of parent expectations.

Insofar as temperament *does* contribute to his tendencies to behave in resistant, disobedient ways, this influence of temperament doesn't excuse your child's unacceptable behavior, nor does it mean you shouldn't work on shaping your child's behaviors. Therefore, we aren't suggesting that you just hunker down, plug your ears, and hide in the bedroom until the child turns eighteen. The temperamentally active, intense child needs extra adult guidance rather than less of it. Although your child has a difficult temperament, he's not destined to be rude, disobedient, and difficult to be around. He may retain a few rough edges here and there, and he may be a bit more at risk for getting involved with alcohol, drugs, and delinquent peers. However, with active, positive, and conscientious parenting, most of your child's harshest edges can be smoothed down, and his risk for developing more disturbing behaviors (covered in the next chapter) can be reduced.

Being defiant is more common in certain ages than others. Folk wisdom has dubbed the toddler stage "the terrible two's" and as usual, there's a grain of truth in the label. Toddlers around the age of two are developing an important sense of self and learning about having limits imposed on them. Some respond more intensely than others to these limits, but almost all respond with occasional dismay or defiance. As toddlers learn that defiance doesn't get them anywhere, they usually begin by using more socially adaptive behaviors to get what they want.

Early adolescence is another time when children more aggressively push limits. Again, the child is in a time of self-development, which involves testing limits and questioning authority. However, the questioning and defiance shouldn't be constant or overwhelming. It shouldn't become the defining feature of the child's personality, even if he's in the throes of hormonal mayhem. And the defiance shouldn't extend to violent outbursts, chronic rudeness, or other forms of severely annoying or threatening behaviors. If it does, strongly consider obtaining a professional consultation.

Getting Professional Help

Sometimes, a child easily meets the definition for oppositional-defiant disorder, but doesn't need professional help because things at home and school are basically tolerable. Other times, a child may not technically meet the criteria, but you know the child needs help. If your child displays four or more of the behaviors listed in the "Signs of a Serious

Problem with Defiance or Anger" checklist on pages 136–137, but you're not sure that professional help is needed, ask yourself the following questions:

- Is my child's behavior really bothering me and disturbing our family life? In other words, is it a big deal?
- Is my child's behavior causing him problems in social, academic, or other important situations?
- Is my child's behavior basically self-destructive? In other words, does his forceful independence cost him in terms of good grades, good friends, good health?
- Am I able to continue to manage my child, despite his defiant behavior, and still maintain a decent relationship?

If you answer yes to any of the first three questions or no to the fourth, your child's defiant behavior is very serious and professional help is recommended.

Many children who are consistently defiant often make their lives more difficult than necessary. For example, one sixth-grade child we know, when asked to throw a piece of garbage in the trash in the school cafeteria, refused, saying, "It's not my trash." When the teacher more forcefully persisted in trying to get him to cooperate, the boy more forcefully persisted in refusing, and threw in a few colorful words to help make his point. Eventually, the principal intervened, only to find herself being subjected to the boy's escalating verbal abuse. In the end, the boy paid for making his point by being cited by the police and suspended from school.

In the preceding case, counseling might help the boy learn to channel his sense of fairness and justice into more promising causes. As noted above, if your child doesn't technically meet the diagnostic criteria, but occasionally blows up or shows other anger or defiance problems, you and your child still might benefit from getting professional help.

Managing a child who's defiant often requires a many-pronged approach. Mental health professionals who specialize in this area will probably work with you, your child, and possibly his school.

There are a few understandable but not-so-smart reasons why you may be reluctant to get help. You may feel a sense of failure or even shame in your inability to control your defiant child. Defiant children are experts in leveling blame. You may feel that somehow your child's defiance is your fault. You may believe there's nothing that can be done. And finally, you may hope that if you ignore the problems, your child will magically calm down and get nicer. Professional help can help you overcome your shame and reclaim your hope.

Most professionals agree that parents should deal with extreme defiant behaviors as early as possible in children's lives with love and firmness. If your child continues to get what he wants by being defiant, then his defiance will probably continue and intensify. Your child might develop new and more extreme ways to be defiant, both verbally, and possibly physically, which will isolate him from the very adults and peers who could help him change.

More Ways You Can Help Your Child

Many parents are unsure about how to react to their child's defiant and angry behaviors. Meeting these behaviors face-to-face on a regular basis can be intimidating. Children with defiance problems don't just push the limits, they shove them, and repeatedly throw their will up against adult authority. Avoid rewarding your child for his defiance inadvertently. This is hard because defiant children are both intimidating and persistent.

In his work with difficult boys, researcher Gerald Patterson of the University of Oregon discovered a family pattern he refers to as a "coercive family process." Dr. Patterson found that this pattern is associated with the development of delinquent behaviors in young boys. Here's an example of coercive family process; it's something to avoid repeating in your family:

Son: Hey Mom, I'm going out to ride my bike with Bobby, we're going down to the little store for some candy.

Mom: No way. You didn't pick up your room or do your homework. You're not leaving here!

Son: You totally suck! I've got the worst family in the world. Everybody else gets to have fun, but you suck. You wreck my life. I never get to have any fun. Do you know how sick you are? I've got lots of time to do my homework. I hate you!

Mom: Oh yeah, well just get out of here then. Go to the stupid store, I don't care!

Son: I'm gone!

As you can see from this exchange, the mom originally set a reasonable limit (although she did so in a rather hostile manner), but then, after her son kept complaining, she backed down. By so doing, she taught him an important lesson. That is, she taught him that through obnoxious persistence, he will eventually wear her down and get what he wants. What this tells us is that your child's obnoxious behaviors may continue because they sometimes achieve the outcome he's hoping for. A child who is defiant, oppositional, and throws temper tantrums when asked to do things may not be required to carry out the task, do his fair share, or comply with requests, simply because everyone gets tired of fighting about it. In such cases the child quickly learns that being defiant and obnoxious works!

You may also be aware of another mistake the mom makes in this scenario. Notice that when she responds to her son's statement, she does so in an aggressive and provocative way. She doesn't just say, "No, honey, I'd like you to pick up your room and finish your homework, and then you and Bobby can go out and have a great time at the store." Instead, the mom actually starts the negativity by responding with her own nastiness to her son's statement about his social plans.

If you think back to the example of Calvin and his mom at the beginning of this chapter, you can see a similar problem. When Calvin, while playing video games, ignores his mother's request, she simply retreats from the situation and then comes back and confronts him with her anger. Then, not surprisingly, Calvin begins responding with his own anger and defiance and the battle rages. In addition, even before their interaction begins, his mom has already endorsed his video game playing by allowing him to have the games in his room (a practice we always discourage because it makes supervising, monitoring, and managing video game play—which can become quite intense—much more difficult for parents).

Like the moms in these examples, sometimes you may be triggering or rewarding your child's defiant behaviors. Be sure to watch out for this unhelpful pattern in yourself. It may be more likely to happen when you're in a bad mood, you've had a hard day, or you're just gearing up for what you expect will be a fight. In almost all cases, a more gentle approach, including loving but firm resistance to rewarding your child's defiance, will gain you more in the long run.

Helpful Hints for Your Child's Defiance and Anger

➤ First and foremost, if you have an independent-minded child, take time to think about your most important family values. Then, talk with friends or other people you respect about how they maintain similar family values. This can help because if your child is consistently challenging you, being clear on your most treasured values lets you know when to stand your ground and when giving in might be acceptable. In other words, figure out how to pick your battles.

➤ Take a parenting class on how to deal with difficult parent-child conflicts, but also consider taking a class on how to listen to and respect your child. This is important because defiant children often react strongly when they think an adult isn't listening to them. Listening well and respecting your child's feelings can help prevent defiance.

➤ Avoid falling into the coercive family process cycle discussed on pages 142–143. This means approaching your child, and responding to his requests, with kindness and gentleness. It also means standing your ground once you've made up your mind or set a limit for your child. Your defiant child desperately needs the firm boundaries he's slamming himself up against. In the process of choosing which rules will hold, make sure the rules are enforceable, and that your child knows the rules and the consequences for breaking each one.

➤ If you say "no" to one of your child's requests and you're having second thoughts, don't switch to "yes" while he's misbehaving. Wait for a calm in the storm. Then, you can switch your decision, as long as the child realized that you've switched your response because you changed your mind and not because he pushed you over. The basic rule is this: If your child is acting aggressively or obnoxiously, the answer is always "no."

➤ Avoid power struggles. If you're clear on what you expect of your child, there's no need to argue. If you're clear on your decision, no amount of arguing will (or should) change your mind.

➤ Look for chances to enjoy your angry, defiant child. If a rare good mood comes by, make yourself available, and play. Do something the child loves. Build your relationship when times are good.

➤ Notice positive behaviors. And give what we like to call *positive character feedback.* This means you should go out of your way to notice when your child is cooperative, instead of defiant, and comment on it. Say something like, "I notice that sometimes you just jump up and do what I've asked you right away. Like last night when I asked you to take out the garbage, you just got right up and did it." Another example: "When you turn off your computer game and come right to dinner when I call you, I feel very happy." It's all too easy to only notice the bad attitude and what isn't getting done, so do your best to focus on positive behaviors when they occur.

➤ Teach and model good anger management strategies. As we suggested at the beginning of this chapter, your child will learn a lot about how to deal with and express anger from watching you. Therefore, it's important for you to work hard at keeping your own angry, aggressive outbursts under control. See the "Check It Out" reading list for suggestions (page 146).

➤ Be flexible and allow the child to have his way sometimes. Listen to his reasoning, and actually change your mind, when he's able to talk calmly and rationally. Don't do this if he's lost it, and is shouting, crying, or hitting things!

➤ Know your child's moods. Don't wade into an unnecessary battle. If steam is already coming out his ears, don't add new irritations. Back off and give him space. Quite often, rest and a good meal—for both you and your child—can be helpful as well.

➤ Try to have predictable schedules and expectations. Implement payoffs and rewards for times when things are going relatively smoothly.

Summing It Up

Angry, defiant children are difficult, exhausting, and sometimes, even frightening. Defiance varies a great deal, both developmentally and temperamentally. However, no matter what the age or personality characteristics of the child, parents have a serious responsibility to help children learn to express anger appropriately, to obey the basic laws of the land, and to develop the skills necessary to conduct themselves in a civil manner.

Seeking professional help, at least in the form of parent education and consultation, can make a big difference. There is no shame in needing help with defiant, angry children. Some parents are handed much more difficult children than others. Recognizing the problem early, and getting help as needed can keep the problem from becoming much worse. Strong-willed, defiant children are challenging, and getting professional help doesn't signal you're inadequate, but rather smart and caring.

Check It Out

Anger: The Misunderstood Emotion by Carol Tavris (New York: Simon & Schuster, 1989). If you're looking for a basic book on anger to help you understand your own and your child's, this is a great choice.

The Defiant Child: A Parent's Guide to Oppositional Defiant Disorder by Douglas A. Riley (Dallas, TX: Taylor Publishing, 2002). If your child shows defiant traits, there are very specific approaches you can use to reduce and cope with the defiance, many of which are included in this book.

How to Handle a Hard-to-Handle Kid by C. Drew Edwards (Minneapolis: Free Spirit Publishing, 1999). Edwards provides numerous positive strategies for helping shape the behavior of difficult or challenging children. Especially recommended in this book is the "Family Problem Solving" section.

Kids, Parents, and Power Struggles by Mary Sheedy Kurcinka (New York: Quill, 2001). Here's a book filled with ideas that can help you manage your child without power struggles.

Raising Your Spirited Child: A Guide for Parents Whose Child Is More Intense, Sensitive, Perceptive, Persistent, Energetic by Mary Sheedy Kurcinka (New York: HarperPerennial, 1992). This is Kurcinka's first book on spirited children. It offers helpful, concrete advice, and it's a favorite among parents who have extra-enthusiastic, energetic, spirited children.

Try and make me! A Revolutionary Program for Raising Your Defiant Child—Without Losing Your Cool by Ray Levy, Bill O'Hanlon, with Tyler Norris Goode (Emmaus, PA: Rodale Press, 2000). You'll find this book informative and fun—but not particularly revolutionary. It also includes some helpful information about how you can keep your own cool instead of blowing up when under parenting pressures.

Chapter 9

Here Comes Trouble: Problems with Aggression, Destructiveness, and Other Serious Behavioral Difficulties

> Nicholas Semicolon was ten years old. He was a husky boy, very strong and large for his age. All parents like to have large healthy children and Mr. and Mrs. Semicolon would have been very proud of Nicholas except for one thing. One shameful thing. Nicholas was a bully. He hit children littler than he was. He teased and hit girls. He teased and hit puppy dogs. He scared cats. He even threw stones at birds and once he tipped over the stroller of a one-year-old baby left outside the grocery store.
> —**Betty MacDonald, *Hello, Mrs. Piggle-Wiggle***

It may be hard for you to admit it if your child is misbehaving badly enough to warrant a label like "bully." It's difficult and sometimes frightening to recognize a cruel streak in your child, or to see a consistent pattern of disregard for others. But it's far better to face facts than to hide from them. Aggressive behavior patterns, like bullying, rarely self-correct, and traditional types of discipline often won't resolve the problem either. In fact, children with these troubles don't seem motivated by quite the same things as other children.

It's 8:30 P.M., Thursday evening. Chase's mother, Chantell, receives a telephone call from his fourth-grade teacher—about Chase again. She feels her skin flush as soon as she recognizes the teacher's voice.

Teacher: Hello, Chantell. I hate to bother you at home again, but I wanted to update you on what's been going on with Chase at school. Has he told you anything?

Mom: Uh. No, I don't think so. Is something wrong again?

Teacher: Didn't he tell you about the playground incident? I told him to tell you about that, and I told him to tell you about what happened in class yesterday, too.

Mom: Well, no. I don't . . . er . . . well, Chase doesn't really tell me much about what happens at school. You know how kids are. I ask him, "How was school?" and he says, "Fine." I ask him if anything happened that I should know about and he says, "Nope."

Teacher: We really need to improve our communication here. Let me tell you what happened. Two days ago, Chase was caught threatening a couple of third graders by one of the playground staff. She overheard him use words that a fourth grader simply shouldn't be using. He was pushing them up against the fence. And we still don't know why.

Mom: Oh, no. We did talk to him about being mean to other children. I thought things had gotten better. I grounded him for a week and he said he was sorry.

Teacher: And the other thing. He stole my best pen right off my desk today. I figured it was him and then I saw him with it and confronted him. Of course, he denied stealing it, yelled at me, and then broke my pen in half and threw it on the floor.

Mom: Oh no. That boy. I don't know what gets into him. I'm really sorry about the pen. We . . . uh, I'll get you a new one.

Teacher: That's all right. The pen's not the issue. The issue is that you've got to find a way to control that boy. Today, I took him to the principal and we gave him a stern warning. Next time he's in trouble, he'll be suspended from school. He was supposed to tell you that.

Mom: But if you suspend him, I'll have to take time off from work. I can't leave him home alone. He terrorizes the neighbors. And he doesn't ever feel the least bit sorry for anything he does and never apologizes. I'm telling you, I don't know what to do.

| Teacher: | Well, I suggest you do something. I think he needs counseling. I've had other parents calling me about Chase. He's the class bully—he even bullies some of the fifth graders. This has got to stop. You need to take some responsibility for his behavior. |
| Mom: | (voice cracking) You don't know what it's like having a boy like Chase. He's a good boy, but he's always in trouble. We keep talking to him. We punish him all the time. What am I supposed to do, stay home with him every day and baby-sit him? Am I supposed to go to school with him everyday to make sure he doesn't pick on anybody? You're always calling me and telling me everything he does wrong. Why don't you call me when he does something right? |

If you have a child like Chase, it's likely that you often feel defensive, worried, angry, confused, embarrassed, and frightened. His behavior problems are more severe than the irritating, but milder oppositional-defiant behaviors discussed in the last chapter. Children like Chase engage in behaviors that violate the rights of people around them. They break rules that hold us together as a community, by bullying, stealing, lying, sneaking away from home or school, destroying other people's property, hurting pets, and so on. And they often don't feel any remorse or guilt for their actions.

What Is Conduct Disorder?

Mental health professionals use the term *conduct disorder* to describe children who regularly act in ways that violate age-appropriate social norms, rules, and laws. If your child has conduct disorder, she's likely to care very little about the rights of others. Her problems probably occur everywhere—in school, at home, and in other social settings. She will have little empathy for her peers and little respect for adults or for rules and laws.

More than anything else, children with conduct disorders get into trouble. Usually they get into trouble because they've stolen something, bullied someone smaller or weaker than them, or vented aggressive impulses toward people, animals, or property. Interestingly, even when caught red-handed doing something wrong, the child with conduct disorder will often lie, blame someone else, or use some other strategy to deny responsibility.

Willy, a twelve-year-old boy was cited by the police for his intimidating behavior at a local bowling alley. As a part of his probation, he was required to attend eight counseling sessions. During his first session, the psychologist, Dr. Vargas, asked, "Hey, Willy, I know what the cops said about the bowling alley, because I got the information from your probation officer. But I'd like to hear from you, what happened at the bowling alley the night you got in trouble?"

"Yeah, okay. Well, I was just at the alley with some friends and I went to get candy and there were these little kids there and I just asked them for some money. That's it." Willy leaned back in his chair.

"Right," said Dr. Vargas. "Okay, so you just asked the kids for some money, then what happened?"

"They gave me some money and I bought some candy and I thought, cool. Then the cops came and arrested me. Those little punks must have made up a story and narked on me."

"So where did the knife come in? I understand, based on the police report, that you had a knife."

Willy squinted. "Yeah, I had my buddy's knife. I had Vince's knife with me, but I never threatened nobody."

"Well, the police report says you held out the knife and threatened the kids and got money from them. It sounds like they thought you were threatening them with the knife."

"Yeah, well, it can't be my fault. It wasn't my knife!"

＊＊＊＊＊＊＊＊＊

Children with conduct disorder, like Willy, typically deny personal responsibility for their misconduct, sometimes in unbelievable and creative ways.

One way to think about the symptoms of conduct disorder is to place them into five separate categories. Consider whether your child's behavior fits into any of the following categories.

Signs of a Serious Problem with Misconduct

❑   My child displays aggression toward people and animals. She often bullies others, starts fights, is mean and physically cruel to animals, and intentionally hurts other people.

❑   My child deliberately destroys property or intentionally sets fires for the purpose of causing damage.

❑ My child is often deceitful and sneaky. She frequently lies to get what she wants or to get out of trouble.

❑ My child steals things from other people or from stores; she may even break into another person's house, car, or property.

❑ My child violates basic rules of conduct for someone her age; she stays out past her home curfew, runs away from home overnight, or is deliberately truant from school.

For most parents, a child engaging in any of the behaviors on the checklist is a major concern. However, if your child has shown at least three of these behaviors within the past year, she's a likely candidate for a conduct disorder diagnosis. For example, if she had tortured an animal, intentionally set a destructive fire, and stolen some valuable items from a store within a one-year period, a mental health professional might label her as having conduct disorder and recommend counseling or other treatment that can help her stop these disturbing behaviors. If your child has been fighting, stealing, and vandalizing your neighborhood, you may have found yourself at wit's end wondering how to manage this behavior. It might well be a relief to discover that she has a diagnosable condition and can get some help.

Oppositional-Defiant Disorder or Conduct Disorder: Which Is It?

As noted in the previous chapter, defiant children are usually angry and difficult to get along with, but they don't tend to cross the line into willful illegal or rule-breaking behavior. They'll yell and scream and swear and call you hurtful names, but they don't torture cats, steal other kids' bikes, set fires to cause damage, or blatantly lie on a regular basis. Defiant kids are exhausting and troublesome, while conduct-disordered kids are usually acting with a malevolent purpose, disregarding the feelings and property of others.

It's not unusual for a child with a conduct disorder to also show oppositional-defiant behaviors, though the two don't always go together. For example, some youngsters don't show anger and disobedience directly. On the surface, they cooperate with rules and get along, but when no one is watching, they steal, lie, and seem to take pleasure in destroying other people's property.

As with oppositional disorder, conduct disorder is more frequent in boys than in girls and is another one of the major reasons why parents or caregivers bring children to see mental health professionals. Conduct disorder behaviors develop somewhat later than oppositional-defiant ones, though in unusual cases, they may begin as early as age five or so. Although your child wouldn't be diagnosed with conduct disorder unless she's been involved in serious misconduct for at least a year, it's important to consider professional help immediately if your child is beginning to show the behaviors listed above. As with oppositional-defiant problems, difficulties with conduct need to be identified and worked with as soon as possible since the longer they go and the older the child, the more deeply ingrained the behaviors become and the harder it is to make positive changes.

Considering Your Child's Age and Temperament

The seeds of conduct disorder are similar to the seeds of oppositional-defiant behavior. Children with these disorders are often, by nature, intense and strong-willed, and their negative moods predominate over positive ones. In addition, school, neighborhood, and family situations can strongly contribute to the development of severe misconduct in children—as in the case of Clifford, described on page 154.

If your child regularly misbehaves, she may have discovered an ugly truth about the world: that is, intimidation, bullying, and other forms of aggression often get you lots of attention and possibly even what you want, at least in the short run. She also may not feel as much empathy, regret, or guilt as most kids do treating other people cruelly. She may cry and wail and pout and do all the things you expect from a normal child. However, when this happens, there are important questions to consider: Does your child feel sad and bad due to feelings of guilt, shame, and empathy for her victim? Or does she feel sad and bad simply because she's gotten caught, and now she'll have to serve some sort of punishment?

If your child has misbehaved and you're wondering what underlies her tears, try not to lead her into answering one way or another, but instead ask something like: "What are you feeling the most bad about?" or "What's really bothering you right now?" If your child responds with, "I'm just sad that I hurt Jamal's feelings and maybe he won't want to be my friend anymore," that shows a healthy development of empathy and conscience. However, if she always only focuses on herself by saying something like, "Having to be grounded really sucks," then it's probably worth consulting with someone who knows a lot about how children develop empathy (a teacher, child development specialist, counselor, or psychologist). You could also try doing some extra reading (see "Check It Out" on page 158) about how to help your child develop more empathy for others.

Children who are aggressive, stealing, and violating the rights of others at an early age usually have a poorer chance for later social success than children who begin misbehaving later in life. Aggression is a tough behavior to change. This may be because, as suggested earlier, aggression is often very effective in getting your child what she wants. Also, it may be because like many children with conduct disorder, your child isn't learning as quickly as most children when she's given external punishments and rewards. In fact, some experts believe that children who regularly engage in misconduct are internally rewarded by the stimulation or excitement of rule breaking, lying, aggression, and other such severely antisocial behaviors. Consequently, when you give your child some punishment, it's actually rewarding because it's just part of the excitement.

How Conduct Disorder Develops

Because children with conduct disorder are so destructive, psychologists have conducted lots of research on them. Although these experts can't say for certain why children develop conduct disorder, they've found that a number of factors in a child's life increase the risk that it will happen.

Conduct Disorder—Possible Factors

Child Factors
- The child has always seemed to have a difficult temperament.
- The child has learning deficits and difficulties (perhaps a learning disorder).
- Naughty or destructive behaviors are displayed early on.

Parent and Family Factors
- There were prenatal and birthing complications.
- Other family members have a history of criminal behavior or psychological problems.
- Punishment by parents is, or has been, harsh or inconsistent.
- The child is not adequately supervised by adults.
- The parent-child relationship is strained and difficult.
- Marital troubles, conflicts, or violence exist in the family.
- The family is living in poverty.

School-Related Factors
- The child and family have little interest or emphasis on academic achievement.
- There is limited teacher availability.
- The teacher rarely uses positive attention or praise.
- Students in the school have poor working conditions.
- There is little emphasis in the school on student personal responsibility.

In addition to the previous factors listed, very difficult neighborhood conditions can contribute to conduct disorder. These conditions might include violence, gang activity, overcrowding, and minimal opportunity for involvement in constructive sports, music, or other community- or faith-based activities. There's also a strong modeling effect; children imitate what they see and so children who see and experience bullying or hurtful behaviors are more likely to mimic these actions.

Clifford, age nine, had endured serious physical abuse from his father as a toddler. His parents had divorced, and Clifford and his older sister had lived in poverty with their mother, moving with her a number of times. Clifford was underweight for his age, but still actively maintained his reputation as a class bully. He'd stolen the classroom pet hamster, cut it up, and froze it in his freezer at home. He'd set numerous fires in garbage cans in his neighborhood—a neighborhood that included rampant gang activity, and was caught starting a fire in the school restroom. Clifford regularly stole money from his mom, and from an elderly neighbor. Clifford was rude, aloof, uncaring, and clearly met the criteria for conduct disorder.

Sometimes a child like Clifford who is misbehaving so severely is both a victimizer and a victim. Clifford had been exposed to many of the family and community conditions that contribute to the development of conduct disorder in children.

Whether or not any of the previously mentioned conditions apply to your child, if she shows signs of a conduct disorder it might be because her attachment to you or other significant caregivers has been seriously disrupted at some point in her life. For example, perhaps you had a long illness that kept your child away from you during infancy, or your child has had repeated changes in caregivers. Attachment disruptions don't always lead to conduct disorder problems, but attachment to caregivers is a powerful and important part of early childhood development. If the attachment isn't steady, loving, nurturing, consistent, and available, the child's emotional, and even physical, development can be hindered. Adopted or foster children are especially vulnerable to attachment problems so if you're raising or working with foster or adoptive children, you can benefit from reading more on this topic (see "Check It Out" on page 158).

Sometimes just getting involved with the "wrong crowd" can cause or reinforce a child's antisocial behavior patterns. Whatever the cause or causes, if you are struggling to understand and raise a child who's showing these troubled behaviors, excessive self-blame is pointless. Instead, you need help. There may, in fact, be some constructive changes that are important for you to make in your parenting or caregiving behavior—but focusing exclusively on your shortcomings isn't helpful. The earlier you get assistance and the more comprehensive the help you get, the better chance you have of making a difference.

Getting Professional Help

As we mentioned earlier, if your child's aggressive, destructive behaviors are allowed to go on regularly after the age of ten or eleven, the problem will get harder to correct with time. In contrast to our emphasis on home-based strategies or interventions in some chapters, here we want to make a strong case for getting professional help, and sticking with it if your child is displaying a regular pattern of misconduct. Getting a clear plan for helping your child to learn more appropriate school and social behaviors—and to abide by the law—is crucial. Several types of help may be advisable—individual or family counseling, collaboration with school personnel, involvement with a probation officer, and possibly a medical evaluation and treatment. You, your child, and society will benefit from early and ongoing intervention.

Professionals who work with conduct-disordered children need both special training and a certain gift for relating to tough kids. When you seek professional help, check around by calling your family doctor or your child's teacher or school counselor, or by talking with anyone else you know who might have inside information on which counselors and psychologists in your community work best with challenging children. Children who show a pattern of serious misconduct tend to be manipulative and are quite effective at pulling the wool over the eyes of inexperienced counselors, teachers, and parents.

More Ways You Can Help Your Child

The old saying "Love is blind" is a particularly dangerous saying for parents who dearly love a child with the severe conduct problems we've described in this chapter. Seeing the best in our children is one thing. Ignoring bullying behavior, theft, lying, aggression, and cruelty is another. If your child has started down this road, it's vital that you not make excuses for your child, that you not shift the blame, not back down, and never stop trying to be a positive influence.

Helpful Hints for Your Child's Misconduct Problems

➤ Provide (or get) extra supervision and monitoring if your child has a tendency to engage in misconduct. Your child will be less likely to display her most devious behaviors directly in front of an authority figure.

➤ Children with conduct disorder problems need firm, consistent consequences. The consequences don't have to be huge, but they need to be important and meaningful to your child.

➤ Children with conduct disorders are masters at pretending that consequences don't matter to them. If your child says, "I don't care," you can bet she does care. If she really didn't care, she wouldn't bother telling you she didn't care. The "I don't care" plea is simply a strategy your child is using to try to get you to give up trying to have power over her.

➤ Don't give up. If your child has this sort of problem, she's probably very persistent. You will need to be even more persistent to keep her in line.

➤ Remember to provide rewards for good behavior, but don't get into the trap of always having to have a reward available every time your child completes even the most trivial positive behavior. Surprise rewards are good. Exciting rewards are good. Large or constant rewards are not recommended.

➤ Don't inadvertently reward your child for negative behaviors. For example, avoid yelling, threatening, or any excessive reaction to negative behaviors. Conduct-disordered children who see us in counseling tell us that they love to see their parents' veins bulging out when they're mad. A good rule to follow is this: Use exciting rewards and boring punishments.

➤ Involve family members, teachers, coaches, and other adults in making sure the message of positive, legal, social behavior is delivered everywhere. Make it clear that mean, hurtful behaviors are absolutely unacceptable. Emphasize that stealing is against the law.

➤ If your child destroys someone's property or steals something, have her go back—even if you have to drag her—to the person who has been offended and make her face her victim and apologize. Require your child to replace the destroyed or stolen item. You will have to teach personal responsibility every day, which means never protecting her from the natural and logical consequences of her behavior.

➤ Take every chance you get to teach empathy. Ask your child how she thinks the other child is feeling. When you see emotionally sensitive responses by television, magazine, or book characters, take a few moments to talk about what you notice and about how the characters may be feeling. Show your own sensitive feelings to your child.

➤ Take a parenting class that focuses on how to set limits and have natural consequences for children who are regularly misbehaving.

➤ Take a long, hard look at your own behavior to see if there's any way in which you may be contributing to your child's problems.

Summing It Up

Children who are aggressive and manipulative, and who disregard the feelings and property of others present one of the more challenging parenting jobs possible. Children with these troubles seem to lack empathy for other people, and often victimize others without remorse. If your child is having problems in this area, it may be for a wide range of reasons, including conditions in her school, neighborhood, family, or herself.

It's important to seek professional help if your child is displaying these troubles, and it's essential that the professional you choose has experience in working with tough, resistant youth. In addition, make sure your child knows the consequences for rule-breaking or destructive, cruel behavior ahead of time, and apply them consistently. It's also wise to reward any positive, kind, or helpful behaviors with the same careful consistency. Children who grow up without interventions for their conduct-disordered behaviors are a costly and sometimes dangerous addition to society.

Check It Out

Building the Bonds of Attachment: Awakening Love in Deeply Troubled Children by Daniel A. Hughes (Northvale, NJ: Jason Aronson, 1999). This straightforward book discusses the problems that can develop when children missed out on the all-important attachment to their primary caregivers early in their lives.

Bullies Are a Pain in the Brain written and illustrated by Trevor Romain (Minneapolis: Free Spirit Publishing, 1997). Learn more about bullying and the pain it causes. This book is a quick read, designed for children who are bullying or being bullied.

Keys to Dealing with Bullies by Barry E. McNamara and Francine J. McNamara (Hauppage, NY: Barron's Educational Series, 1997). This book is geared toward parents and teachers. It provides examples and guidelines for effectively reducing bullying behaviors.

Rage-Free Kids: Homeopathic Medicine for Defiant, Aggressive, and Violent Children by Judyth Reichenberg-Ullman and Robert Ullman (Arlington, VA: Prima Communications, 1999). For a nontraditional, homeopathic approach to calming down angry and violent children, read this book.

Winning Cooperation from Your Child: A Comprehensive Method to Stop Defiant and Aggressive Behavior in Children by Kenneth Wenning (Northvale, NJ: Jason Aronson, 1999). Here's a basic guide for dealing with misconduct in younger children.

Chapter 10

Unusual & Severe: Other Problems Requiring Professional Help

> A horse and a flea and three blind mice
> Sat by the roadside shooting dice.
> The old horse slipped and fell on the flea.
> The flea yelled, "Whoa, there's a horse on me!"
> **—Anonymous**

Children present challenges parents never dreamed they'd face. Sometimes the hardest challenge is to admit that you don't know what to do.

When faced with a child who acts in highly unusual and disturbing ways or isn't developing normally, you may feel as small and overwhelmed as the flea in the opening poem. Asking for help can seem embarrassing, especially if your child is behaving in ways that are strange and scary to you.

We hope this chapter can help you identify and cope with some of the more extreme problems your child might have. In previous chapters, you learned about the most common problems of childhood that warrant professional attention. In this chapter, we'll discuss some difficulties that are more rare, are potentially quite serious, and typically require professional help.

Unusual Language, Movement, and Social Difficulties

The famous scientist Albert Einstein was very slow as a child to learn to talk. The same is true of many very intelligent adults. So having a child who's a bit slow in developing the ability to say and use words isn't necessarily a major cause for alarm. However, speech and language therapy can be very helpful for children who are quite late in developing their ability to talk.

As a general rule, check with a speech and language specialist if:

- by age two, your child hasn't or won't use spoken language
- by age three, your child isn't using short phrases to communicate with you.

Sometimes children with mild to severe language problems also show other unusual behaviors.

Sander, a very attractive, but nearly nonverbal three-year-old boy was brought to counseling by his parents. Among other unusual behaviors, Sander had a very peculiar obsession with keys. Even before he was a year old, he clung to keys as if they were teddy bears or pacifiers. He kept them with him at all times and became very distraught if his keys weren't around. Sander had toy keys, real keys, small keys, large keys . . . and he stroked them and cooed to them rather than actually trying to unlock things with them.

≈‡≈≈≈‡≈≈■

Between birth and three years, if your child shows any of the symptoms on the following checklist, arrange for a *developmental assessment* by a pediatric or developmental specialist at the earliest opportunity. This assessment will determine if your child needs special help with learning to speak and related problems. Your pediatrician can help you with referrals to the right specialist.

Signs of a Serious Problem with Language, Movement, or Social Play

❑ My child can't or won't use appropriate nonverbal social behaviors such as eye contact or common communicative gestures.

❑ My child has lost ground with regard to motor development or has never progressed in terms of normal motor development.

❑ My child has not shown an interest in having any meaningful peer relationships.

❑   My child has a marked inability to use language appropriately; he says the same words repeatedly in ways that are very unusual for a child.

❑   My child shows a lack of spontaneous sharing, spontaneous make-believe play, and social play at a developmentally appropriate level.

❑   My child shows a marked preoccupation with very narrow and unusual objects or activities.

❑   My child engages in repetitive physical mannerisms such as hand flapping or odd movements of the head and limbs.

Some of the problems on the checklist may be noticeable within your child's first year. Others may not show up until age two or three. In either case, getting an assessment as soon as you become aware of these problems is important. It may be that your child is just showing some unusual variations on what's normal. On the other hand, the symptoms listed are often associated with a set of conditions called *pervasive developmental disorders.* The most common of these disorders are *autism* and *Asperger's syndrome.* Sander, the boy in the previous story, is showing a symptom of autism—a very intense and narrow focus on an unusual object. If you think your child has developmental symptoms, consult with your pediatrician right away to arrange for a thorough evaluation.

Learning Disabilities

If your child's ability to learn in school is well below his intellectual potential, he may have a learning disability. We won't describe all the various learning disabilities, but if you have concerns about how well your child is learning in school, an assessment by a specialist in learning disabilities can help determine if your child needs special help. As part of the assessment process, your child's achievement level (how much he's learned in school) and his intelligence will be tested. If his achievement test scores show he is performing significantly below his intellectual potential, he may be diagnosed with a learning disability. Children can have learning disabilities, also called *learning disorders,* in reading, mathematics, and written expression.

At home, you can watch for the behaviors on the following checklist that might signal a learning disorder.

Signs of a Serious Problem with Learning

❑ My child has a strong negative reaction to studying that goes beyond the normal resistance many children show. For example, he makes loud and persistent protests that give the impression it's actually emotionally, and almost physically, painful for him to study.

❑ When my child does study, the concepts just don't seem to sink in. For example, he may put in long periods of time studying and then completely flunk the test he was studying for.

Of course, even if your child shows these signs it doesn't necessarily mean he has a learning disorder. In many cases children naturally resist studying, and sometimes children flunk tests even though they've studied hard. Usually, flunking despite studying hard is because of test anxiety and not a specific learning disorder. You might also check yourself to see if you have unrealistic expectations about your child's school accomplishments, a common problem among parents. You may believe your nine-year-old should be reading the classics when, in reality, he's only interested in the comics—which is actually a good sign, because at least he's reading something. However, if you take into account any unrealistic expectations you have and still believe your child is having unusual trouble with learning in school, review the "Helpful Hints" list that follows for some steps you can take to help your child.

Helpful Hints for Your Child's School Learning Problems

➤ Attend your child's school parent-teacher conferences (this is good advice for all parents).

➤ Let him know—in a kind, not nagging, way—that you're interested in his school performance and that you expect him to try his best.

➤ Strive to be an active participant in the teaching and learning process. Provide a neat, quiet space for reading or studying.

> Gently check in with your child about homework assignments and determining if your assistance is needed (but, if he asks for help, remember to just sit by and help—don't get impatient and do the homework for him). Communicate regularly with the school regarding your child's performance and progress.
>
> ➤ If, at any time, you suspect your child is having big difficulties in reading, reasoning, math, writing, or remembering basic school-related information, ask his school for a formal meeting to discuss the problems.
>
> ➤ If it seems warranted, request testing or observation by the school psychologist. Don't be shy about exploring these issues; it's your right to have your child tested by the school.

If your child has a learning disorder, be prepared to be assertive in getting the assistance your child needs. An estimated two to ten percent of all school-age children suffer from learning disabilities. This means your school personnel are often busy and overwhelmed just covering the basics. Therefore, if you don't make sure your child receives the extra help he needs, there's no guarantee someone else will find the time and energy to make sure he gets it.

Severe Eating Difficulties

While the causes are far from understood, a small percentage of children repeatedly eat nonfood items. Examples include eating dirt, paint chips, insects, gravel, and even feces. Obviously, if your child eats these types of things, it's quite disturbing.

We're not talking about the normal oral phase all children go through, during which they'll put things in their mouth that make even the most stout-hearted of us cringe. Normal oral exploration is just a common way for your child to get to know the world. Even this can be a stressful time for you as parent, because you can't turn your back for a second without fearing that your otherwise normal and intelligent child will start picking up and popping disgusting or poisonous items into his mouth.

If your child regularly eats one or more nonfood items and keeps this up for more than a month, this is a cause for special concern. However, you may decide, as many parents do, to seek professional assistance even if your child is only occasionally eating such substances. We recommend you err on the conservative side. If you have the least bit of concern about your child's unusual eating behaviors, make a telephone call to your local hospital or medical center for more information.

Other disturbing eating difficulties include: when babies or toddlers refuse to eat; when they eat, but then throw the food right back up; and when they regurgitate and then re-chew their food. Any of these eating behaviors, if continued repeatedly, can result in weight loss, electrolyte imbalance, or in failure to gain normal amounts of weight. These patterns can represent a very serious problem. If you notice these problems even a few times, a visit to the doctor is in order.

Tics

In the movie *What About Bob?*, Bill Murray, as the lead character, talks about the tic disorder he has. He shows many common motor and vocal tics, such as eye blinking, neck jerking, facial grimacing, shrugging (motor tics), and throat clearing, grunting, sniffing, barking, snorting (vocal tics). Of course, in his usual comic style, Murray displays these symptoms with great vigor and humor. In contrast, if your child shows the symptoms of a tic disorder, you likely won't find them the least bit funny. And realistically, no one should blame you; tic disorder symptoms are puzzling, embarrassing, and sad.

Occasional tics are not unusual, but if they persist, occur frequently, and seem beyond your child's control, then take him to a doctor for an evaluation—especially if your child has been acting this way for a month or more. If your child experiences vocal and motor tics together or exhibits more complex tics, such as uncontrollably shouting obscenities or jumping and stamping, serious intervention is needed.

Some medications that are commonly prescribed for attention deficit hyperactivity disorder can produce tics in children or adults. These medications include, but are not limited to Ritalin, Cylert, Dexedrine, and Concerta. Also, medications designed to control psychotic symptoms, such as hallucinations (see the following section) can cause a permanent condition involving mouth or tongue twitching, known as *tardive dyskinesia*. Our main point is that if your child has any odd movements while on a psychiatric medication, check with your doctor about possible side effects and continue to observe your child's movements closely.

Hallucinations

Children sometimes have imaginary companions. This is partly because children have wonderful, active imaginations; their imaginations help them fulfill social and emotional needs in novel, creative ways. We recall with some fondness an eight-year-old girl who insisted to us that dragons were just as real as humans. She also greatly preferred playing "pretend" over any other activities. Fortunately, this particular girl—our youngest daughter—lived in her imaginary world only part-time, and was able to function well in the real world of school, soccer, and family life.

In contrast to the imaginative child, some children actually begin seeing, hearing, or smelling things that no one else can see, hear, or smell. If this is happening to your child, he may be having *hallucinations*. Hallucinations are much different from playful imagination in two important ways:

- Hallucinations are real sensory experiences—they're not imaginary or pretend.
- Hallucinations are usually undesirable—most often they consist of insulting or bossy voices that tell children mean or scary things.

If your child has hallucinations, at any age, it warrants your concern. Talk with a physician or mental health professional. Contacting a professional immediately is especially important if your child is hearing voices that are saying mean or scary things. Immediate help is important because, in extreme cases, children who hallucinate also become suicidal.

Although hallucinations may signal psychological problems and usually require a professional assessment, there's one situation when hallucinations are considered normal. If your child hallucinates when dropping off to sleep, during sleep (as in dreaming), or when he's just beginning to awaken, he's probably experiencing normal sleep-related hallucinations. There's usually no need for professional consultation about these hallucinations, unless they're occurring very frequently and your child is extremely upset when they happen.

Tendencies Toward Violence

In Chapter 5, we talked about how to respond if your child acts suicidal or tries to hurt or harm himself. Sometimes, though, destructive impulses are directed outward. Following the spate of school shootings in the late 1990s, parents, teachers, and most adults who spend considerable time around children have become sensitized to children who speak or act in murderous or threatening ways. If your child repeatedly expresses a wish to hurt or kill others, your concerns are justified.

Children regularly exposed to violence learn that violence is a possible solution to irritants in their lives. This is a consistent message received by many children through television, video and computer games, and violence-oriented toys, games, and sports. Researchers have linked heavy viewing of violent images on television and in video and computer games to violent behavior. Children growing up amidst street violence also may be more prone to using violent means to get what they want. Recently, we heard of an extreme example of how effectively violence can be taught to young children. A colleague who does research in war-torn countries told us of a child who was raised his entire five years in a combat situation. His father, a soldier, brought his son into an emergency nursing station for an immunization. When the nurse administered the shot, the boy yelled in pain, and then said, "Daddy, this woman is hurting me. Why don't you kill her?"

Although it's impossible to accurately predict whether a single child will commit a violent act, you should watch for the symptoms described in Chapter 9 on pages 150–151 as well as those on the following checklist.

Signs of a Serious Problem with Violent Tendencies

❑ My child has threatened other children or hinted about engaging in violent acts.

❑ My child carries weapons, initiates fights, and engages in vandalism or animal cruelty.

❑ My child is preoccupied with violent fantasies, movies, games, music, or weapons.

❑ My child feels rejected, bullied, humiliated, or mistreated by his peers. (This can be a problem sign, as nearly every school shooter to date has said his motive was to seek revenge for repeated social humiliation and rejection.)

> ❏   My child has made direct statements about wanting to hurt or kill someone.

Impulse Control Problems

Imagine yourself with a ten-year-old child who, upon being asked to help with garden weeding, explodes into a rage and begins smashing a shovel against the side of the garage. A very small number of children act impulsively and aggressively in this manner with powerful intensity. These responses come out of nowhere. Typical types of outbursts include rage, physical attacks, verbal assault, destructive fire setting, or other dangerous actions. If your child seems prone to such outbursts, he may have *intermittent explosive disorder.*

Intermittent and disproportionate explosive responses to minor incidents can be shocking to you and other family members. In response to such outbursts, sometimes you may feel forced to "walk on eggshells" or "tiptoe" around the house, fearing your child might explode at any moment. As you can imagine, most parents eventually conclude that this isn't the way family life was meant to be, and wisely seek professional assistance.

Another rare impulse problem that warrants treatment goes by the imposing name, *trichotillomania.* This condition involves the repeated pulling out of one's hair, resulting in significant hair loss. While some people might find the thought of hair-pulling so odd that it seems silly, this problem is far from humorous. Children who suffer from it feel out of control of their hair-pulling, and patches of missing hair cause significant social distress.

Upon successfully pulling out hair, children with trichotillomania generally experience pleasure, gratification, or relief. The act appears to relieve tension for them. If your child is pulling out hair from his head, eyebrows, and eyelashes, contact a professional who has experience with impulsive or obsessive behavior problems. This specific impulse-based problem typically responds well to behavior modification.

A twelve-year-old girl was referred for counseling after she began pulling out large chunks of her hair on a regular basis. She also had pulled out all of her eyebrow and eyelash hairs. At the time of counseling, she was ashamed and embarrassed by her appearance. She was extremely relieved to find out that other children struggle with the same problem. She cooperated with her therapist and learned to relax her body, reduce her nervousness, and keep herself from hair-pulling if she felt the urge to do so. Within six months, her hair grew in and she looked and felt normal again.

꙰꙰꙰꙰꙰꙰꙰꙰

Two other impulse-based disorders deserve brief mention here. If your child often steals things or sets fires, but doesn't appear to have any other significant problems, he may have *kleptomania,* a compulsive tendency to steal things he doesn't need, or *pyromania,* a compulsive tendency to set fires. He may describe this impulse as "irresistible." These puzzling patterns require treatment.

Panic Attacks

Panic attacks are less severe and more easily treated than other conditions in this chapter, but their intensity is overwhelming and they can be very disturbing for you and your child. Panic attacks consist of sudden periods of intense fear or discomfort that come about unexpectedly. During these periods, physical symptoms can include increased heart rate, sweating, chest pain, nausea, and shortness of breath. An especially disconcerting, but common, part of a panic attack is the fact your child may believe he's about to die, or that he's going crazy. Obviously, these thoughts and beliefs tend to intensify the feeling of panic.

Sometimes panic attacks begin after a frightening or near-death experience. One adult we knew began having panic attacks after an allergy attack swelled her throat shut and nearly killed her. It took a year of counseling and medication assistance for her to get over her attacks. Both adults and children who have panic attacks often feel ashamed and frightened. If your child experiences panic attacks, he may reduce his social activities out of fear that he'll have an attack in front of people. As you can see, this can become a vicious cycle. Breaking the cycle of fear requires skilled professional help.

Panic attacks seem to come out of nowhere. If your child experiences a panic attack, he will feel like his body is under siege and become very scared. However, it may not be apparent to anyone else that he is having a problem. Give him reassurance that he's not alone, and that he's not "crazy." Counseling, sometimes combined with medication, is usually very effective in helping children control feelings of panic.

Obsessive-Compulsive Disorder

From time to time, we all get a tune stuck in our heads or we find ourselves doing something over and over that seems silly. Before long, we usually do stop whatever we're doing and don't give it much more thought. Children with obsessive-compulsive problems have the same tendency to repeat what can seem like the silliest things, only they're not able to stop themselves.

The mom of a ten-year-old girl telephoned our office, asking for advice on a problem her daughter was having. She explained that her daughter had begun digging at a certain spot on her cheek, making it bleed every day. Even further, she said her daughter told her, "If I make my cheek bleed once a day, Grandma won't die." A few brief questions about this girl's behavior revealed a pattern of anxiety, followed by ritualistic behaviors, including the cheek problem, but also repeated counting, checking, tapping, and hand washing—all designed to fend off bad events. We advised the mom to take her daughter to see a psychologist in town who specialized in the treatment of obsessive-compulsive disorder.

There are several books available to parents of children suffering from obsessive-compulsive disorder (see "Check It Out" on page 174). These books help parents understand the peculiar and repeated thoughts (obsessions) and behaviors (compulsions) engaged in by their children. Behavior modification, medications, or a combination of these two treatments can help children who have this debilitating problem.

Alcohol and Drugs

Consider the following questions:

- Do you think it's possible for preteen children to have serious problems with drugs?
- Did you experiment with or abuse tobacco, alcohol, or other drugs when you were a teenager, or even younger?

We ask these questions because your own attitude toward alcohol and drug use will greatly influence whether you believe smoking cigarettes and drinking alcohol is normal, or a potential problem, for your child. If you used alcohol and drugs sometime during your youth, you may think it's completely normal for children to do a little "experimenting." On the other hand, if you mainly remember how much trouble or pain your own use caused you, you may be very worried about your child's potential for drug abuse.

Many parents believe that, for the most part, serious alcohol and drug problems begin during the teen years. Unfortunately, this isn't accurate. Although alcohol and drug addiction problems are huge during the teen years, more serious alcohol and drug problems actually begin during the preteen years or even earlier. Recent research has shown that the brain of a younger child is more susceptible to drug addiction than the teenage brain. Of course, this doesn't mean that if you manage to keep your child from experimenting with drugs before he reaches his teen years, then your drug prevention job is over. However, generally speaking, the younger a child starts using drugs, the more likely he is to suffer severe emotional, behavioral, and psychological problems such as depression, delinquency, and anxiety throughout the rest of his life.

At age nine, Miguel began smoking cigarettes. Shortly after turning ten, he and some buddies started huffing (inhaling) whatever substances they could find that might give them a quick "high." They experimented with paint thinner, gasoline, glue, and fumes from aerosol cans. By age eleven, Miguel was regularly getting alcohol from teenagers in his neighborhood and he started smoking pot every day during recess at his middle school just before he turned twelve years old.

Of all the possible problems your child might eventually face, problems with alcohol and drugs top the list. This is because far more children experiment with alcohol and drugs than have problems in any other single category discussed in this book. Also, children who have many of the other problems described in this chapter and elsewhere in this book, use and abuse alcohol and drugs in an effort to relieve themselves from their painful symptoms. When unsupervised by parents or other adults, young children are often at risk for using tobacco, alcohol, marijuana, and inhalants. Not surprisingly, the type of drugs your child may be exposed to will vary depending upon where you live. If you're curious about what drugs are most likely to be abused by children in your area, ask your local health department about this important bit of information.

As illustrated in Miguel's case, very young children are often at greatest risk for abusing inhalants and tobacco. Both inhalants and tobacco are often considered "gateway" drugs, because their use tends to lead to further drug experimentation, abuse, and eventually, drug dependence. Inhalant abuse, sometimes referred to as huffing, can include the inhalation of glue, gasoline, kerosene, aerosol cans, paint, or other substances in an effort to get "high." As you can imagine, your child might have access to many inhalants in your home and neighborhood. Inhalants are powerfully mind-altering, and overuse can result in unconsciousness or death.

When your child takes the leap from elementary school to middle school or junior high school, it becomes much more likely that he will be offered tobacco, alcohol, and other drugs by his peers and older children. For example, in many areas, about one in five (20 percent) seventh graders has tried smoking marijuana. Without a doubt, the risks for drug use and abuse are out there—even for very young children.

For older teens and adults, occasional use of drugs, alcohol, and tobacco is often considered normal. In contrast, because of the vulnerability of the developing brain, any use of a mind-altering substance among preteens and younger children is a cause for serious concern. Substance abuse prevention professionals suggest that you restrict your child to "no use" of alcohol and other substances at least until age fifteen. Additionally, if you provide or allow your young child to use substances, both you and he will be breaking the law and serious legal consequences are possible.

The main possible exception to this "no use" rule involves ceremonial use of substances. For example, it may be acceptable for your child to have a sip of wine as part of a wedding toast or during a bar-mitzvah celebration. Similarly, American Indian youth might be permitted to use tobacco during a culturally sanctioned ceremony. Otherwise, most professionals agree, children fourteen years old and younger should not be allowed to use drugs.

As a parent, you're probably nervous or scared about what drugs your child will be exposed to in your neighborhood or at his school. If so, the best thing you can do to reduce the chances of your child using drugs is to develop and maintain a close relationship with him. You can do this by working hard on communication, spending time with him, and letting him know how much you love him. It's also important for you to let your child know that you don't want him to experiment with dangerous drugs.

Even though it's impossible to always know where your child is and what he's doing, it's important for you to keep very close tabs on his daily activities. For example, we recommend that you ask your child to check in with you regularly to tell you where he is and what he's doing. Of course, your child will probably resist your efforts to monitor his behavior, especially as he gets older. He may complain that you don't trust him or that "all my friends get to stay out later than me!"

Of course, it's important to give your child many choices among healthy and positive activities he can do with others, and to give him more and more freedom as he gets older and is able to handle it responsibly. However, regularly monitoring and supervising your child's activities will help you keep your eyes, ears, and nose tuned in to the signs of drug use problems in the following list.

Warning Signs of a Serious Problem with Drugs or Alcohol

❑ My child's eyes are sometimes red, glassy, or dilated. He sometimes overuses eyewash to cover-up eye irritation.

❑ Unusual smells, such as chemical breath, are noticeable. Sometimes my child uses too much cologne or mouthwash to cover up these smells.

❑ There's been a marked change in my child's appearance or hygiene.

❑ My child has had an unexplained weight loss.

❑ My child has been emotionally explosive and verbally abusive to me or other family members.

❑ My child's speech is sometimes slurred.

❑ My child has had drug paraphernalia among his belongings.

❑ My child's school grades have suddenly dropped, and so has his motivation to do other things normally important to him.

❑ My child has been stealing things or coming home with valuable possessions that he won't explain how he got.

❑ My child has repeatedly lied or acted in sneaky or deceptive ways.

If you observe one or more of the drug abuse warning signs in your child, discuss what you're seeing with trusted friends or family. Also, an initial professional consultation can help you determine your best course of action. This action may involve getting additional education or counseling for you and your child. We recommend that you participate fully in counseling with your child to help you stay closely involved in his life and to show your genuine concern. Try to avoid following through on the impulse to drop your child off with a counselor to "get fixed." Your participation is crucial.

Getting Professional Help

If you've read this entire chapter, by now you may be feeling a bit overwhelmed. The problems we've talked about are unusual and severe, and therefore, can be very disturbing to you as a parent.

In many of the previous chapters, if your child is affected by the problems described there, we've recommended that you contact your local health department, consult with your child's doctor, or schedule a counseling appointment for you and your child. Our advice for the problems in this chapter is similar, but more urgent. Each of the problems listed in this chapter calls for early intervention. Without the aid of counseling or medical treatment, they can develop and progress into even more severe conditions.

Deciding what type of professional to talk with about your child's problem is especially difficult with the problems described in this chapter. We'll explain in detail in the next chapter how to choose a professional. For now, keep in mind that choosing the right professional for the especially severe problems in this chapter requires some background research (rather than just a quick glance through the yellow pages). Calling your local mental health center or hospital is a good place to start. Ask for names of professionals who have experience working with children and specialize in your child's particular problem. Again, we'll discuss the entire issue of getting professional help in greater detail in the next chapter.

Summing It Up

It's scary to think about, but it's possible for your child to suffer from a number of unusual and severe mental, emotional, or behavioral problems. These problems include autism, learning disorders, severe eating problems, tics, hallucinations, violent tendencies, impulse control problems, panic attacks, obsessions and compulsions, and problems with alcohol and drugs. Although dealing with these problems can feel overwhelming, it's possible for you to help your child deal with each problem discussed in this chapter. Finding the right professional who can work effectively with you and your child is crucial.

Check It Out

Asperger's Syndrome: A Guide for Parents and Professionals by Tony Attwood (London: Jessica Kingsley Publishers, 1998). Including comments from parents and patients with Asperger's syndrome, this book provides relevant and useful information on all aspects of this unusual problem.

Behavioral Intervention for Young Children with Autism: A Manual for Parents and Professionals edited by Catherine Maurice, Gina Green, and Stephen Luce (Austin, TX: Pro-Ed International, 1996). This book instructs parents and professionals in how to choose effective treatments for autism and on how to implement a behavior modification plan at home and at school.

The Boy Who Couldn't Stop Washing: The Experience and Treatment of Obsessive-Compulsive Disorder by Judith L. Rapoport (New York: The Penguin Group, 1991). This is an excellent book to help you understand and manage childhood obsessive-compulsive disorder.

The Explosive Child: A New Approach for Understanding and Parenting Easily Frustrated, Chronically Inflexible Children by Ross W. Greene (New York: HarperTrade, 2001). This book is specifically written to address problems with children who regularly explode in anger.

Freeing Your Child from Obsessive-Compulsive Disorder: A Powerful, Practical Program for Parents of Children and Adolescents by Tamar E. Chansky (New York: Crown, 2001). There are a number of very specific strategies available for helping children overcome their obsessive-compulsive behavior problems. This book will tell you how to use these scientifically-tested strategies.

Help for Hair Pullers: Understanding and Coping with Trichotillomania by Nancy J. Keuthen, Dan J. Stein, and Gary A. Christenson (Oakland, CA: New Harbinger, 2001). It's great to find a book to address your exact need, and here's one that clearly describes the problem of hair-pulling and methods for gaining control.

Just Say Know: Talking with Kids About Drugs and Alcohol by Cynthia Kuhn, Scott Swartzwelder, and Wilkie Wilson (New York: W. W. Norton, 2002). This book gives parents and teachers ideas for talking with kids about the dangerous effects of alcohol and drugs on the young mind and body. It focuses on a wide range of different drugs and suggests conversation strategies.

A Mind at a Time: America's Top Learning Expert Shows How Every Child Can Succeed by Mel Levine (New York: Simon & Schuster, 2002). If you have a child with a learning problem, this book can give you hope and clear techniques for helping your child overcome his problems and succeed.

Chapter 11

The Wide World of Professional Help

We were sitting in a makeshift kitchen where the staff crowded in for lunch. The speaker was Laotian. A Hmong co-worker placed a straw basket packed with "sticky rice" in the center of the table; a Japanese counselor added short-grained rice from a rice cooker; a Chinese American clinician added a bowl of long-grained rice. The different varieties of rice silently spoke to the different philosophical, ethnic, cultural, historical, and religious traditions represented around that table. And yet we were all considered to be "Asian." Both viewpoints contain aspects of the truth.
—**Christina Chao, *We Do Not Even Eat Rice the Same***

What kind of rice do you like best? What kind of rice does your child prefer?

Like the counselors in the opening quote, your preference and your child's preference for rice may be related to your particular ethnic and cultural background. But also, you and your child are unique. You may be a mom of African lineage, a dad with a Jewish heritage, or an American Indian grandmother, but at the same time you're different from other African moms, Jewish dads, and American Indian grandmothers. You have unique tastes, philosophies, and family traditions when it comes to the choice and eating of rice.

As you gaze into the wide world of professional help, you may find yourself feeling a bit confused by all the differences you see. That's understandable. Just as there are many different types of rice and rice preferences based on various cultural perspectives, there are many different types of mental health professionals, each with its own particular philosophies and traditions. There are also individual differences based on the unique experiences and strengths of each professional. Plus, when choosing a professional, you have your own background and personal preferences to consider as well!

Think of this chapter as mainly a menu describing the many types of professional help available for children who have emotional, social, or behavioral problems—and for their families. By becoming familiar with the various choices on the menu, you'll be better equipped to decide what sort of help best fits your personal needs and preferences.

First, we'll introduce you to the main ways that mental health professionals go about helping children. Then, we'll describe each of the types of professionals you can choose from, and their training and credentials. In this chapter you'll also find some ideas on how to decide which professional to see, advice on figuring out how to pay for services, and suggestions concerning the assessment and diagnosis process. This chapter will be your guide through the basic steps of getting professional help.

The Basic Steps for Getting Professional Help

1. Gathering Information About Different Professionals and Their Services
2. Figuring Out How to Pay for Services
3. Deciding Exactly Who to Go See
4. Dealing with Assessment and Diagnosis Issues

Gathering Information About Different Professionals and Their Services

In earlier chapters, we've mentioned different sorts of mental health providers who might be able to help you and your child.

Now it's time to give you more information about these various types of professionals.

Types of Professionals to Choose From

At least five main types of mental health professionals provide services for children or families with emotional or behavior problems. These include:

- clinical social workers
- counselors
- psychologists
- psychiatrists
- psychiatric nurses

In addition to these five main mental health providers, there are other professionals who offer mental health related services as a minor part of their overall services, such as:

- clergy
- physicians with specialties other than psychiatry
- teachers
- naturopaths
- speech and language specialists
- physician's assistants
- tribal elders and healers in Native cultures

For personal reasons, you might prefer to consult with someone in this second list, but usually children's mental health issues aren't primary specialties for this group of professionals. Therefore, we'll limit our discussion to clinical social workers, mental health counselors, psychologists, psychiatrists/physicians, and psychiatric nurses.

Types of Credentials

As you begin to select a mental health professional for your child, an important issue for you to know about is professional credentials. Professionals in mental health can be *licensed* and *certified*. In this chapter, the discussion of licensing and certification of mental health providers pertains to procedures used in the United States. However, if you're not residing in the United States, you can still follow the basic rules outlined here. In particular, because most countries have consumer protection laws, before you decide to take your child or family to a mental health provider, check for regional or national licensing or certification. Additionally, most countries also have national professional organizations, for example the Canadian Counselling Association or the British Psychological Society, that can offer you guidance in determining which professional is right for your situation.

In most states in the United States, mental health professionals are required to have a state license to independently offer professional services. For example, a counselor must be licensed in New Jersey if she wants to legally offer private counseling services in New Jersey. This same counselor cannot legally offer services in New York.

Mental health professionals can also be certified, usually by a national organization, as having particular expertise or competence. For example, nurse practitioners can be certified by the American Nurses Association or the American Academy of Nurse Practitioners. Similarly, the National Board for Certified Counselors certifies counselors and the Board of the National Association of School Psychologists certifies school psychologists.

Some different mental health professionals obtain a separate credential for counseling people with addictions or chemical dependency problems. Nurses, counselors, social workers, and psychologists often choose to have this additional certification. The exact name of this certification varies from state to state. The important thing to remember is that you can ask mental health professionals about their training and their credentials to practice, and they should provide you with answers that make sense and make you feel secure about their skills, training, and credentials. The credential question is also important if you have health insurance, because your insurance company or health maintenance organization may only cover some costs if you see a credentialed professional.

Now that we've reviewed some basic information about mental health credentials, let's take a closer look at the five individual types of providers. These different types each have distinct educational backgrounds overall, yet may have some overlapping training, skills, and philosophies. For example, one clinical social worker can be more similar to a psychologist or psychiatrist than she is to another clinical social worker. Even central characteristics, such as professional degrees, don't necessarily distinguish the day-to-day practices of mental health professionals, but the following descriptions should be generally helpful.

Clinical Social Workers

Sometimes, social workers are stereotyped as intrusive or even antagonistic representatives of "the system" because of their work as child advocates in adult and child welfare agencies. Social workers who provide individual counseling, however, have a very different function and focus than child welfare social workers. Don't be fooled by narrow and inaccurate stereotypes; not every social worker sees her primary role as child protection.

Although it's possible for people to get a doctorate in social work (D.S.W.), in most cases, a social worker who provides mental health counseling will have a master's degree (M.S.W.). This means most social workers have training that's on a par with other master's level providers in counseling and psychology, who are described later in this section, and their philosophy and treatment approaches are also similar. (See pages 184–185 for more information on the letters you might see following the names of mental health providers.) Of course, if you decide to seek counseling or therapy services from a person with a master's degree in social work, make sure that person is licensed by your state or regional governing body. You can find out this information by asking the professional or by contacting your state licensing board. If your state doesn't have social work licensing, ask the professional if she has a national social work certification.

Counselors

There are many kinds of counselors. Although some counselors have doctoral degrees, most counselors who provide mental health services have master's degrees in particular counseling specialty areas. Some specialties include:

- school counselors
- community or mental health counselors
- marriage and family counselors

School counselors are trained to work with problems your child might have in the school setting, especially problems that get in the way of learning. You may remember your own school guidance counselor as someone who helped you decide whether to go to college, or what to do after high school. College and career guidance is still an important function of the school counselor, but many are now also trained to provide counseling for mental health and behavioral difficulties.

The philosophy of your child's school and the school counselor's personal interests dictate the services the school counselor provides. Many school counselors are too busy to regularly provide individual counseling for children. Your child's school may have as many as 400 children served by one school counselor. However, if your child has a relatively minor, school-based problem, such as shyness or aggression on the playground, consider contacting the school counselor to see what services are available. Occasionally, school counselors provide social skills groups, divorce adjustment groups, depression groups, or very brief individual counseling to students in need. School counselors can also provide you with excellent information about a good professional for your child to see in your community. School counselors are usually certified, but are not typically licensed by the state to provide mental health counseling services outside your child's school.

Community, mental health, and marriage and family counselors are usually licensed by state governments to practice counseling, meaning she at least has the minimum level of knowledge, training, and experience required by that state. Often, the license includes the word *professional,* or similar to social work, the word *clinical,* as in licensed clinical counselor. Sometimes, counselors identify themselves as mental health counselors, to distinguish their training from other kinds of counseling training. Other times, counselors identify themselves as marriage and family counselors. These professionals work primarily with couples and families, rather than individuals. As discussed in many of the preceding chapters, your child's problems may be best addressed by having your whole family go see a family therapist or counselor.

Community, mental health, and marriage and family counselors are very similar in their role and function. They're usually in private practice, or they work for agencies or clinics. If you seek services from a counselor, ask whether this person is licensed to provide counseling services in your state. If your state, province, or region does not license counselors, ask if your counselor is nationally certified.

Psychologists

There are also many kinds of psychologists. The types most likely to help with children's serious problems like those discussed in this book are:

- school psychologists
- clinical and counseling psychologists
- neuropsychologists

Not surprisingly, *school psychologists* work almost exclusively in schools. They're specially trained to give your child intellectual and academic achievement tests. These tests can tell you whether your child has a learning disorder. Generally, school psychologists don't offer individual counseling. Most are certified by the National Association of School Psychologists, but are not licensed as psychologists, although individuals who receive additional training may become licensed as a counselor.

Clinical and counseling psychologists have training similar to mental health counselors or clinical social workers. However, in most states and regions, individuals can't call themselves psychologists unless they've obtained a doctoral degree and are licensed to practice psychology.

If you take your child to see a psychologist, she'll probably have more training in the following areas:

- providing psychological assessment
- diagnosing children and adults
- working in a medical or hospital setting
- providing services to children with severe emotional and behavioral problems.

The difference between a counseling and clinical psychologist is small. For the most part, counseling psychologists are trained to offer services to individuals with less severe problems. But, as is the case with mental health professional degrees, the philosophy and focus of practice of individual psychologists is based mostly on the psychologist's professional preference.

If you take your child to see a psychologist, she's a little more likely to get a type of counseling or therapy that is highly structured and scientifically tested. This more rigorous, scientific approach can be appealing, especially if your child is suffering from a specific disorder, such as obsessive-compulsive disorder, attention deficit disorder, or conduct disorder. Generally speaking, psychologists are more likely than any other type of provider to have you or your child complete assessment questionnaires prior to beginning therapy.

Neuropsychologists provide extensive testing services to children and adults. These services focus almost exclusively on neurological or brain functioning. Neuropsychological testing helps with diagnosing specific problems with learning, processing information, or paying attention. Neuropsychologists also must be licensed to provide services in your state or region. You're most likely to benefit from the assessment services of a neuropsychologist if your child has:

- a head injury
- a puzzling array of symptoms
- a learning problem
- attention deficit hyperactivity disorder symptoms

Psychiatrists

Psychiatrists are medical doctors trained to treat mental disorders. They've completed medical school and can prescribe medication. They're often employed in medical settings, hospitals, or in private practice, although a few work in community mental health centers. Of course, anyone who achieves doctoral level training can call herself "Doctor," so don't assume you're seeing a psychiatrist just because the person has "Dr." in front of her name. If you're not sure about what type of degree your child's "Dr." has, be sure to ask.

Psychiatrists are the only mental health professionals with medical degrees. This means they:

- have extensive knowledge and training about physical health and illness
- can put "M.D." after their names
- spend much of their training focusing on biology and medicine and less on providing therapy or counseling
- can prescribe medications

A few psychiatrists get extensive mental health training beyond biological or medication management and become further qualified to provide psychotherapy or psychoanalysis. You can ask about any additional qualifications a psychiatrist has, if you wish to see this doctor for counseling.

If you think your child has a condition that might benefit from medication treatment, most often your best bet is to take her for an appointment with a child psychiatrist. However, because of the biological-medical philosophy of most psychiatrists, taking your child for an appointment greatly increases the chances that treatment will include medication. Also, if you live in a small community, it may be difficult to get an appointment with a reputable child psychiatrist. That means you may need to turn to a different provider type to obtain a medication prescription.

Pediatricians, neurologists, or other physicians sometimes provide assessment or professional services for children with mental health problems and may be willing to prescribe medications for your child. Also, in New Mexico and in the military, psychologists are legally able to prescribe medications after completing training. No matter who prescribes, remember that your child's body-mind connection is an intricate one, so if she is receiving medications from a licensed provider, that provider should closely monitor the medication effectiveness and side effects to assure your child's safety.

Psychiatric Nurses

Although most nurses practice under the supervision of physicians in hospitals, clinics, and other medical settings, some nurses independently provide counseling or psychotherapy to individuals, couples, and families. Some have received graduate training in mental health counseling and psychiatric treatments. If you are considering a psychiatric nurse who works in private practice, check for both a state nursing license and national certification as a nurse practitioner. This helps assure that the treatment provided, whether medication or counseling, meets national or regional practice standards.

What the Letters After Their Names Tell You

In the phone book, or in other advertisements or listings, professionals indicate their academic degrees and licenses or certifications. Listed on pages 184–185 are the various abbreviations or letters you're likely to see connected to your mental health provider.

The Letters After a Professional's Name

THE LETTERS YOU SEE	WHAT THE LETTERS MEAN
M.A.	A master of arts degree. Be sure the degree is in counseling or psychology and not history or some other irrelevant field.
M.S.	A master of science degree. Again, check for relevance.
Ed.D.	A Doctor of Education degree received from a university's School of Education. Professionals with an Ed.D. are also usually licensed as counselors.
Ph.D.	A Doctor of Philosophy degree received from a department of psychology or counseling at a university. Most psychologists have a Ph.D.
Psy.D.	A Doctor of Psychology degree received from a professional school of psychology. Some psychologists have a Psy.D.
M.S.W.	A master's degree in social work.
D.S.W.	A Doctor of Social Work degree received from a university's School of Social Work.

L.P.C. or L.C.P.C.	A Licensed Professional Counselor, or Licensed Clinical Professional Counselor designation. These titles usually indicate that the counselor does mental health counseling.
L.C.S.W. or L.S.W.	Licensed Clinical Social Worker, or Licensed Social Worker designation. These titles usually indicate that the social worker does mental health counseling.
C.C.D.C.	A certification in chemical dependency counseling. There are many state-by-state variations for this designation.
M.D.	A Doctor of Medicine degree received from a medical school.
R.N.	A Registered Nurse degree from a School of Nursing.

There are so many abbreviations, and it can become quite confusing. Never be afraid to ask what the letters stand for. You're the consumer and it's your right to understand your mental health professional's background, training, certification, or licensing status. If you meet a professional who misrepresents his or her professional background or status, report this person to your state licensing board.

Specialty Training

Many mental health professionals develop specialties. You might see children mentioned as a specialty—or specific problem areas or diagnoses such as drug addictions, anxiety disorders, and so on.

Matching the symptoms you're seeing in your child with practitioner information might help you narrow your list. Often, providers will list their special interests, approaches, or expertise in the descriptions of their practice.

To claim a specialty, a professional should have extra education or training in a particular area. Some graduate schools focus exclusively on certain problem areas, treatment techniques, philosophies, or ages. Medical doctors and psychologists both have options for board certification in specialty areas, but often, professionals develop special expertise in an area without pursuing actual certification. In counseling and social work, exact standards for listing these specialties is less regulated, so it's up to you to ask about whether a particular provider has experience with problems similar to what your child is displaying.

Unfortunately, we've seen mental health professionals advertise levels of experience that would have taken 50 years or more to obtain. Of course, exaggerated advertising is unethical, but it does occur. This is one reason why we generally advise against selecting a mental health professional from the yellow pages of your local phone book without also gathering information from teachers, school counselors, your insurance provider, your child's physician, or friends about the professional's reputation.

Figuring Out How to Pay for Services

Mental health services for children and families can be very expensive, but sometimes, it's possible to get reduced fees, or even free services. For example, at our parenting clinic in Montana, because of grants that underwrite our services, we can meet with parents for a sliding fee scale that can go as low as $5 and can provide free information to parents over the telephone. At the other end of the spectrum, out-of-pocket costs to parents can be $150 or more for an office visit.

Check Your Budget

Consider the expense of mental health services the same way you consider other important purchases you make. Before you contact a mental health professional or agency, look over your budget and think about what you can afford to spend each week or each month for services. If the services are exceptionally important or necessary, you may decide, as you would with other important purchases, to obtain a loan or to use a credit card to finance crucial mental health treatment.

Check Your Insurance Coverage

As you calculate what you can afford to pay out of your own pocket, take a look at whether you have health insurance to cover a portion of your mental health treatment expenses. Most states require insurance companies to provide coverage for mental health conditions. For example, your state may require your insurance company to pay 50 percent of mental health expenses, after a deductible. "Deductible" is one of several terms you will want to be familiar with as you explore how much coverage your insurance company will provide:

- *Deductible:* If your policy has a deductible (let's say $500), you'll pay the first $500—the deductible amount—and your insurance company will pay all or part (let's say 50 percent) of any further expenses.

- *Reasonable and customary fees:* The insurance company may only pay 50 percent of what they have determined are "reasonable and customary fees" for the services, regardless of what the provider actually charges.

- *Preferred providers:* Your insurance company may have a list of preferred providers, in which case they will pay a higher percentage of the costs if you choose from this preselected list.

- *Gatekeeper system:* Many insurance companies have a gatekeeper system, meaning that you need approval or authorization from your primary doctor before you go for counseling; otherwise the counseling will not be covered by your policy.

If you're enrolled in a health maintenance organization (HMO) or have a managed care policy, you may:

- have to pay a small co-payment for mental health services (about $5 to $20).

- have to abide by strict rules that require authorization before you can receive services, and limit who you can see and how many visits you can have.

Whether you have a more traditional health insurance plan, an HMO, or a managed plan, it's important to check all the rules in advance to make sure you're doing everything correctly before you make an appointment. It can be very frustrating and disappointing to find out that your insurance plan won't pay anything for services you received because you didn't get the proper authorization or that you went to the wrong provider. In almost every case, insurance companies require that you or your child be diagnosed as having a mental disorder for coverage to take effect.

The best way to find out exactly what your insurance company or HMO will pay for is to closely read your policy literature. Then, because insurance companies often use their own peculiar language, it's a good idea to call or meet with an insurance company representative to make sure you understand your personal benefit package.

Check for Medicaid or Medicare Coverage

You may not have any insurance coverage and may have very little money to spend on anything other than food and shelter. If so, contact your local, state, or regional assistance office to see if you qualify for Medicaid coverage. Medicaid is a federally-funded insurance program, but each state can implement it differently. Usually, your local Office of Public Assistance or your City or County Health Department can provide you with information about how to become eligible for Medicaid coverage. Your local Office of Public Assistance can also help you find out if you're eligible for disability or Medicare coverage.

Check for Free or Low-Cost Community Services

You may have very poor health insurance coverage or no insurance coverage, but still have an income too high for you to qualify for state or local support. If so, your choices are limited, but here are a few ideas:

- Find out if your child's school offers any counseling services or parenting classes for people in your situation.

- Ask your child's school administrator, school counselor, or school psychologist if they have recommendations for low-cost counseling in your community.

- Check with the human resources office where you work to learn if your employer offers counseling through an employee assistance program.

- Call your City or County Health Department and ask if they have a list of mental health providers who see children and families for free or for a small fee.

- Contact your county or regional mental health center. Often mental health centers will offer services for a reduced rate.

- Check to see if your community has local nonprofit organizations that offer parenting classes or private parenting consultations. You can probably get this information from your local Department of Child and Family Services or your City or County Health Department.

- Contact providers listed in the phone book under Counselors or Psychologists and ask if they will accept clients on a "sliding fee" or donation basis. This means the professional is willing to reduce fees for people with limited incomes. If you find someone from the phone book who agrees to do so, you may want to check with your child's school or other people in-the-know to make sure you've selected a reputable provider.

Deciding Exactly Who to Go See

As we discussed previously, licenses, degrees, and certifications are important. They insure, to some extent, that your mental health provider has the academic and professional training necessary to offer services. However, there are many other concerns you may want to consider before choosing a professional.

Therapy or Counseling?

There are at least four main words commonly used for the help people seek from mental health professionals. These words are *counseling, therapy, psychotherapy,* and *psychoanalysis.* In addition, occasionally professionals will use the word *consultation* to describe the services they're offering. So, for example, if you and your spouse or partner decided to work on your relationship because doing so might benefit your child, the person you see might be called a couple's counselor or marriage therapist. Also, the person that might suggest you come for an initial consultation might refer to his office as the "consulting room."

Counseling, therapy, or psychotherapy have much in common with each other, as well as some subtle differences. In this book, we've used counseling and therapy interchangeably, and left out the term psychotherapy, because it generally refers to a longer-term process that isn't used with children. The fourth term, psychoanalysis, has a more specific meaning. When one is undergoing psychoanalysis, the sessions usually occur several times a week. The professional providing the service is a credentialed psychoanalyst, and has undergone specialized training for many years to provide this type of service. Such treatment is expensive, lengthy, and not usually recommended for the kinds of problems most children develop.

Medication Issues

Physicians will be your primary source for psychiatric medication prescriptions. Pediatricians, family practitioners, and internists can prescribe psychiatric medications, but if your child's problem is fairly complex, psychiatrists or neurologists are more likely to manage these medications.

Medication is often prescribed for attention deficit hyperactivity disorder. It's also prescribed for depression, and sometimes, to help with severe obsessive-compulsive behaviors. However, these medications don't always help, may have serious side effects, and in some cases, have not been well tested for use with children.

You don't need to go directly to a psychiatrist simply because there is a *chance* that medication will be a consideration. This is a topic you should talk over with whatever mental health professional you choose. Your mental health professional can help you sort out various treatment options, with medication as one possibility. In our opinion, other treatment options should be tried first, with medication reserved for problems that don't improve with individual or family counseling or with behavioral management.

Professional Reputation

Gather as much information as you can about whoever you're considering. Ask around in your community; friends, teachers, physicians, clergy, or others might have important knowledge or experience to share. Children, especially teens and preteens, sometimes talk with each other about professionals they've seen and liked (or hated). This can be important information to consider as well. If your child thinks a particular counselor is "cool," the chances of a positive outcome may be enhanced.

What to Consider When Calling or Interviewing a Professional

Before you call for an appointment, it's a good idea to make a list of questions you'd like to ask. One of the most important factors to consider when working with a mental health professional is the goodness-of-fit between the professional and the client or family. Make sure you and your child feel good about working with your selected professional. Some reasonable questions to ask a potential therapist include:

- What's your professional training and background?
- Do you have a particular specialty?
- How much do you charge for your services?
- How long are the sessions?
- What times do you have open for appointments?
- What is your usual approach to working with children?
- Will you include parents or the whole family in the meetings?
- Have you worked with many children who have problems similar to my child? (You might specifically ask about experience with bedwetting, ADHD, childhood depression, anxiety, or whatever problem your child is struggling with.)

When asking professionals about their background and experience, they might be a bit defensive or curt with you. Since the effectiveness of counseling and mental health work is related to the relationship you have with the professional, this isn't a good sign. Of course, just as you might decide to go see a physician with a great reputation, but lousy bedside manner, you might decide to make an appointment anyway. However, we believe you have a right to ask these important questions (ask politely, of course) and to have them answered in a caring, professional manner.

Relationship Potential

If you have the time and money, it's not a bad idea to schedule a brief meeting with a professional you're considering, before you make the final choice. You might even ask for a short interview with your top two or three choices. This isn't uncommon, but it can be expensive and a bit of a hassle. You can also gain lots of information by talking with the professional on the phone. Usually, you can ask to just visit for fifteen minutes to get a better idea about how she might work with you and your child. The extra time you take to get a sense of the professional's orientation and approach might pay off in the end. Here's why:

Helping people with emotional and behavioral problems is both an art and a science. Professional education provides the "science" part; but the artistic part comes from the practitioner's ability to form a trusting, caring, ethical relationship with the client. If you don't feel a connection to the professional, it's far less likely that she'll be effective in helping you or your child. We also believe your child needs to feel a connection to the professional—although not necessarily the first time the two of them meet. As we'll discuss in the next chapter, children rarely volunteer to get professional help. You need to give it some time, but if, after three or four meetings, you, your child, or your family find it difficult or impossible to relate to the professional, you may need to move on.

Practicalities

Most counseling sessions last 50 minutes, although sometimes during the first visit, an appointment may be longer. Professionals in private practice will have you fill out paperwork about problem areas and basic background information. They'll also ask for financial information for insurance billing. Some of them will accept Medicaid payment and some will not. Some of them will have a sliding fee, based on your income, and some will have a standard fee. If you're seeking help from an agency, such as your Community Mental Health Center, a public clinic, a hospital, or a nonprofit community-based child and family counseling service, the paperwork and payment expectations may be slightly different, and you may be placed on a waiting list. Some religious bodies also provide counseling services to members and may request specific types of information from you or have other requirements.

What Do Mental Health Professionals Actually Do?

The first thing mental health professionals typically do when you bring your child for help is to perform some sort of assessment. This may involve talking to you and your child, filling out questionnaires, having your child draw pictures or tell stories, or even gathering information (only with your permission) from teachers and others who know your child. It's important that the professional gets some clear, working hypotheses about what's going on with your child and what might help. Sometimes, professionals just ask a series of questions to help them better understand the situation. If you're curious, ask your provider what assessments she uses and why.

Let the mental health professional know that you want to understand any diagnosis she gives your child. Arriving at a diagnosis is important because:

- It helps narrow down treatment options.
- It can be a relief for you to find out your child's problems or troubles fit a pattern that other children have experienced and recovered from.
- It's an efficient way for professionals to communicate with each other so they can best help your child.

Your child's diagnosis will be shared with your insurance company, if you have one, and become part of your child's medical record.

If your counselor uses questionnaires or other assessments, ask about the test results. The assessment results may give you insight into your child's personality or coping style. They may also help with treatment choices. And, just as important, they may not seem accurate to you. This is crucial information. Psychological assessments aren't perfect. They're based on statistical norms, and can sometimes be a bad fit for a given individual. Discuss with your mental health professional any doubts you have about the diagnosis or assessment results for your child.

Assessment is an ongoing process. However, after getting a general idea about your child's difficulties, the professional will begin working with your child, or your family, on the problem areas. There are many different theories, techniques, and approaches for working with childhood troubles. Professionals consider theory, technique, problem areas, and other factors in determining what to do. That's why they go to graduate school and get all those credentials. There are many treatment options, some of which we mentioned in each of the chapters of this book. Common therapy approaches or techniques that mental health professionals might use with your child are briefly described below.

Cognitive Therapies

There's no question that the ways your child thinks about herself, her world, and the future affects her emotional state. Of course, her emotional states, school circumstances, and family environment affect the ways she thinks as well. It's very much a chicken-and-egg situation. However, it may sometimes be easier to teach your child to think in new ways than it is to teach her to feel differently. Therefore, for some problem areas, having your child learn new thinking—or *cognitive*—strategies will be the main goal of the counseling. Besides talking with the therapist, your child may be asked to do some reading, keep track of her thoughts during the week, and use other methods to help her make a change in her thinking.

Behavioral Therapies

People like rewards. We tend to repeat behaviors that get us what we want and avoid or stop those that don't, or those that have negative consequences. A professional who uses behavioral therapies may help your child—and you—change troubling behaviors by changing reward and consequence systems. Also, the therapist may teach new behaviors to help with certain troubles. Learning to relax and meditate is a good example. Children who learn to calm themselves down and chill out can master certain anxious moments, and can begin overcoming phobias and other disturbing fears.

Similar to the way cognitive therapists work, behavior therapists are also very likely to have your child practice dealing more effectively with difficult situations. However, rather than have your child focus on what she's *thinking* during these difficult situations, the behavior therapist will mostly just help your child *practice some healthy reactions* to the situation over and over. Behavior therapists believe very much in the virtues of practicing very specific social and physical skills.

Play and Less Verbal Therapies

Some children are chatterboxes and enjoy talking—even talking about their problems. However, others don't find talking nearly as easy or enjoyable. A professional working with your child will probably have art supplies, small sandboxes, toys, puppets, or games available to help establish a relationship and gain an understanding of the problems. Sometimes, the puppet interactions or the games may include a direct therapeutic message about new ways your child could use to handle problems. Other times, they will provide an atmosphere for talking that achieves similar results. Either way, both play and art activities seem to facilitate healing and change. They are especially helpful with children who have experienced significant trauma. It's been shown that children who have been exposed to big stresses or trauma are helped by having a chance to work through their emotional reactions using play.

Family Therapies

Many kinds of counseling involve parents, siblings, or other caregivers occasionally in the process. However, some professionals believe the best (or even the only) way to really help a child is to work with the whole family to change things so the child is no longer experiencing the distress, or acting out the troubles that have been identified. Depending on your child's troubles, it might be worth talking with at least one professional who does primarily family work, just to get a perspective on how that might help.

Not all family therapists will use the same approach to helping children. However, most family therapists have the same general goal—to help all family members improve their relationships with one another, usually by using more direct and positive communication within the family.

Primarily Relationship-Based Therapy

All therapy involves a caring relationship. If that doesn't exist, not much else matters. But some professionals believe that change most likely occurs *because* of a caring, therapeutic relationship, especially in certain problem areas. These counselors might use techniques from the other therapies listed above, but their basic belief is that a child can sort out her troubles best in the context of a relationship that is private, respectful, and caring.

Unlike behavioral and cognitive therapists, a relationship-based therapist isn't likely to tell your child what to do. Instead, because of this belief in the natural healing qualities of a deeply personal relationship, the therapist will listen to your child and play with her. In some ways, the therapist acts like a mirror, reflecting back to both you and your child what she's seeing and then allowing the two of you to make changes you desire as a result.

So What Should I Do with This Information?

Just as it isn't the parent's job to diagnose, you also can't be expected to know which theories or techniques are best for your child's troubles. That's where developing a good partnership with your mental health professional comes into play once again. Feel free to ask your provider questions about the best form of treatment available for your child. Use the following questions or make up your own. You'll notice that some of these questions are similar to those we suggested you use when selecting a professional. Once you've chosen someone, you'll want to revisit some of these areas in great depth.

- What form of counseling or therapy do you provide?
- What form of counseling or therapy do you think would be best for my child?
- Do you think family therapy might be helpful?
- Is the therapy you provide based on a particular theory? If so, which theory?
- Will you be using cognitive or behavioral approaches to teaching my child new behaviors?
- What new behaviors do you think my child needs to learn and how can I make sure what I'm teaching her at home is consistent with what you're teaching her here?
- Will you be using play therapy with my child?
- Is the therapy you provide based on scientific research?
- What books or articles should I read to help me know more about the type of services you'll be providing for my child?
- What can I do at home to help my child benefit most from your services?
- How many sessions will it take before I start to see improvement in my child?

The purpose of asking these questions is to make sure you're fully informed about the type of counseling or therapy your child's provider is offering your child. It will also help you understand what to expect as counseling progresses, giving you some idea of both the timeline involved and what sorts of signs of improvement you can watch for.

Summing It Up

When you choose a mental health professional, consider the following:

- training and background
- specialties that suit your child's needs
- professional reputation
- relationship potential—how comfortable you and your child are with this person
- affordability and how you will pay for services.

When you make the call, have questions ready. You can interview one or more professionals before making your final decision about who to see. At any time, feel free to ask your child's or your family's mental health professional questions about testing, diagnosis, treatment types, or techniques your professional is using. Helping children with problem behaviors usually requires a team approach, and you're a central part of the team.

Check It Out

One way to get a sense of the differences between various types of mental health professionals is to visit the Web sites of their professional organizations. Here we've listed Web sites for several of these organizations, most of which also provide some consumer information. Also included on the list are sites that don't represent an organization but offer lots of practical information about mental health issues and services.

www.4therapy.com
This Web site is designed to help consumers of mental health services understand and find the help they need. It includes helpful information on different types of mental health treatment and strategies for finding a therapist.

www.aacap.org
This is the Web site for the American Academy of Child and Adolescent Psychiatry. It includes some helpful information for parents including "Facts for Families," questions and answers about child and adolescent psychiatry, facts about gun violence, and a glossary of symptoms and mental illnesses affecting teenagers.

www.mentalhelp.net
Here you'll find information about a wide array of mental health related services and issues such as insurance reimbursement, mental disorders, finding a therapist, and self-help alternatives.

www.apa.org
The Web site of the American Psychological Association offers information about psychology, children's self-help books, as well as referral resources, including a toll-free number, 1-800-964-2000, to help you find a psychologist in your area.

www.counseling.org
This American Counseling Association site includes a "Counseling Corner" that has articles written for the public and articles on ethics for counselors.

www.naswdc.org
The Web site for the National Association of Social Workers offers information on advocacy, including the NASW code of ethics, publications, and how to contact members of congress to support particular legislation on issues related to social work.

www.schoolcounselor.org
The American School Counselor Association has specific information for parents on its site, plus a bookstore.

www.nasponline.org
Here's the site for the National Association of School Psychologists. It includes information on "What is a school psychologist?" and helpful handouts each month on different topics like "bedtime" and "sleepwalking in children."

www.aabt.org
You'll find useful science and other facts on this Web site for the Association for Advancement of Behavior Therapy. This organization specializes in providing information about mental health treatments based on scientific research. You'll find fact sheets and a clinical directory and referral service.

www.ispn-psych.org
This Web site for the International Society of Psychiatric-Mental Health Nurses has great links to other helpful Web sites for parents.

Chapter 12

Here You Go!

> When facing a difficult task, act as though it is impossible to fail. If you're going after Moby Dick, take the tartar sauce.
> —**H. Jackson Brown Jr.,** *Life's Little Instruction Book*

Making the Decision to Get Help

Now that you have the information about how to get professional help, it's up to you to make a decision about whether to go ahead and set up an appointment. For some parents, this decision is very difficult. It can be agonizingly hard to know whether or not you, your child, or your family needs professional help. As a general guide, if you answer yes to any of the following questions, it might be time to go see a professional.

- After reading the chapters that address the main concern you have about your child in this book, are you still as worried as you were when you began reading?

- Have you tried some of the helpful hints included in this book, but your child's behavior isn't improving, or is getting worse?

- Is your child's behavior or emotional state interfering with his ability to participate in activities normally expected for his age and you don't have hope for improvement?

- Do you have a nagging feeling that your child's behavior or emotional state is unhealthy and a belief there's someone out there who can help him?

Even if you answer yes to all four of the preceding questions, you still may not want to go for professional help. That's okay. As a parent, you have the right to try to handle things at home. On the other hand, sometimes even a short visit with a mental health professional can give you helpful ideas and a sense of direction. Also, keep in mind that the decision of whether or not your child goes for help is a family decision; you'll need to talk with your child's other caregiver and your child about possibilities for getting help.

Involving the Other Parent

Here's one big dilemma you might face: What if you think your child needs professional help, but your child's other parent or main caregiver disagrees or, even worse, is philosophically opposed to counseling of any sort? This is an especially difficult question if you've been through a divorce or permanent separation and you and the other person are living in separate homes.

Whether you live with the other parent or not, good communication about this issue is important. Try to bring up the topic in a direct, but hopeful way. You might say something like, "I'm very worried about Garrett. He's been fighting on the school playground again and he doesn't have any friends. And you know what he's like at home, especially in the mornings. He's so grumpy that both of us are afraid to say anything to him. I think we should consider counseling for Garrett, or maybe we should meet with someone to see if there's anything more we can do at home. I love Garrett and I know you do, too. With some help, I think he could do better at school and start feeling better about himself."

If your suggestion is met with resistance, you might try asking a few questions. But avoid confronting the other person with questions like, "What's wrong with taking Garrett for counseling?" You'll probably just get a defensive response. Instead, ask questions that bring you together as a team for your child.

- How do you think we can help Garrett do better at school?
- What do you think might help at home?
- If we don't take him for counseling, how would you feel about you and I visiting with the school counselor or Garrett's teacher to get more information and make a plan to help him?
- What other options, besides counseling, would you suggest we pursue to help Garrett?

If you've brought up the issue and asked team-oriented questions in a sincere and respectful manner, and the other parent is still opposed to considering counseling, you could try making a joint plan for *how* to decide when to turn to counseling in the future. You could say: "All right, I can tell you really don't want Garrett to go for counseling right now. I respect that. You also don't want to talk to anyone at school because you're worried that might draw too much negative attention to Garrett. I'm worried about that, too. So, instead of going to counseling or talking with the school right now, how about we try using the helpful hints in Chapter 5 in this book for the next three or four weeks? Then, if Garrett's not doing any better, you and I go together and talk with a counselor about what's been going on with Garrett and see what the counselor has to say. Okay?"

Finally, if the other parent is against getting help for Garrett no matter what, you may need to take matters into your own hands. Tell the other parent politely and sincerely about your plan, and then, out of your concern and for your child's health and well-being, go ahead with your decision to take a child to see a professional.

Considering Your Child's Concerns

Of course, along with discussing this important decision with the significant adults in your child's life, you'll need to talk with your child. Chances are, your child won't beg—or even ask—you to take him to a mental health professional for help. He's more likely to resist the idea of going. Most kids don't even like routine doctor or dentist visits, and they especially hate the idea of going to counselors, psychologists, and psychiatrists! There are obvious reasons to resist visits to a medical doctor or a dentist—namely, shots and fillings. However, his reasons for resisting mental health visits may be more subtle and numerous. Here are examples of concerns your child might have:

- He may not be aware of the significance of his emotional and behavioral problems. If your child tends to be irritable, defiant, or hurtful, he may blame others for the way he acts. It's everyone else who has the problem, not him. If he has internal troubles, such as anxiety and depression, he may assume all children feel the way they do, and not see himself as deserving or needing help.

- He may not be aware that help is available and may believe he just has to live with things the way they are.

- He may feel deeply ashamed and not want anyone to know about his struggles.

- Professional counseling or therapy normally involves at least some talking, and your child may not enjoy sitting around talking—especially about his problems. He's more likely to want to move, play, draw, run, sing, tease, and, in general, interact physically with his world. The "talking cure" may hold little appeal for him, especially if he assumes that counseling simply means talking (or even worse, being talked to) about very emotional and uncomfortable topics.

What If Your Child Asks for Help?

If your child proves us wrong, and actually does ask to talk with a professional, gently inquire about what he'd like to get from counseling. You don't have to grant his request instantly, but take his concerns, and his request, seriously. If you're uncertain about how to respond to your child's request, consult with teachers, your family physician, the school counselor, or trusted friends and family before making a final decision.

What If Your Child Doesn't Ask (But You Wish He Would)?

Most likely, you'll be the one to decide that your child (or you) should meet with a mental health professional. If you decide to go on your own, whether to gather information or to improve your parenting, you can do so discretely, perhaps without telling your child. Alternatively, if you decide to take your child for an appointment, you'll need to consider how best to tell your child about your decision.

The Resistant Child

If your child's problems are more on the acting-out, resistant side, you can probably expect opposition to counseling. However, if possible, try to find a way to sidestep a direct power struggle. Any attempt to force your child to go should be your last option. If he buys into the idea of going to counseling—even just a little bit, he's more likely to benefit from the process. Also, it will make the counselor's job that much easier if your child isn't coming in feeling hostile because he lost the fight with you. We've had more than a few children come to our office who were so angry about coming to counseling, they said things like, "I'll never speak to you, and you can't make me!" If your child reacts like this, there's no need to be overly concerned though, because experienced mental health professionals can usually handle resistant kids. Our main point is this: if you can sidestep the power struggle over going to counseling, all the better.

Tips for Avoiding a Power Struggle with Your Child About Going to Counseling

➤ Try to find out your child's biggest concerns or complaints about seeing a counselor. Your child may be resisting because of embarrassment, or feelings of personal failure, or fear. Once you've learned why your child is resisting, you can do your best to address his concerns and see if that helps.

➤ Present the idea of going to counseling as something that's cool, rather than something that's negative. Say something like, "Hey, we're a smart family and so when we have something we want to improve, we go to someone who can help." Besides that, you might want to point out that lots of movie stars have their own counselors.

➤ Try making a deal. If your child agrees to go for help and give counseling a fair chance (say, three visits and some honest interactions with the counselor), then you agree to provide a reward, grant a coveted freedom, cook a favorite meal, or do something else special that will help motivate him. Some parents object to this approach, saying that they're against bribery. While we understand the concern these parents have about over-relying on rewards as a way to get a child's cooperation, it's helpful to remember that, even as adults, we all appreciate incentives—on the job, for example—to motivate us when we face a tough or intimidating task. In addition, it's important to remember that the real meaning of bribery is to pay someone, usually in advance, to do something illegal. Of course, there's nothing illegal about taking your child to counseling. When you offer your child a small incentive or reward for going to a counselor and cooperating, you're using effective behavioral management strategies.

➤ If you want to be less direct about providing an incentive, think about it this way: We have many wise parents who bring their children to us after school and who, on the way to the counseling appointment or afterwards, take advantage of this natural opportunity to spend quality time together and to stop for a snack, meal, or visit to the park along the way.

➤ Try giving an alternative to counseling. Clearly identify the troubling behaviors you are concerned about. Give your child the choice of changing the behaviors in very measurable, significant ways in a defined block of time (perhaps one or two weeks). If the changes are successful, then no counseling is indicated. More likely, the troubles won't go away that easily, and you'll have proven your point that the child is struggling and can more easily insist the child come to talk with the professional.

➤ Try giving your child a choice about the type of counselor or counseling. For example, ask him, would you like to see a man or a woman for counseling? Or would you like to see a cool counselor or a nerd counselor? Or, would you like to go for three meetings or six meetings? By providing a choice, you also provide your child a sense of control—which tends to feel better than coercion.

➤ Find someone who can tell your child that he or she went to counseling and that it wasn't too bad and that it helped.

➤ If these first seven strategies fail, then you might have to resort to the power parent approach. There comes a time (actually, there come many times) in the careers of all parents, when standing firm and insisting on the right thing *is* the right thing to do. You recognize that as the primary adult responsible in your child's life, you are responsible for making critical decisions about his welfare. Just as you'd find a way to get him to a dentist—no matter how resistant he might be—if he had a mouthful of cavities, when he clearly has a need for counseling, you're also his best source of support and the final authority for his well-being. Ironically, children who protest mightily at the time may later—perhaps many years later—thank the parent for having the courage to stand up to the protests and insist on a course of action. If you're convinced your child needs professional help, find a way to get him to go.

The Anxious Child

If your child is generally anxious and high-strung, he'll likely feel nervous about talking to a stranger. Reassure your child that you'll be there, and will help explain the troubles. Do your best to make the whole idea sound both normal and safe.

Tips for Preparing Your Anxious Child for Going to Counseling

➤ Make a clear plan with your child for how to cope with going to counseling. For example, you might say, "First, we'll get ourselves ready to go. If you're feeling nervous, we can take your favorite CD or tape in the car and listen to it on the way. Then, we can go into the office early and wait, or wait in the car until the last minute, whichever you'd like. When you go in, I'll be there and you can hold my hand and squeeze it all you want, but I'll wait for you to grab it. Then, after the meeting, we'll go to the park and swing on the swings and relax."

➤ Try to model or demonstrate calmness and strength as you carry out the plan. Remember that your child takes his biggest cues from you.

➤ If your child has a favorite book, toy, or stuffed animal, suggest bringing it along, and assure him that the counselor or psychologist will be interested to know about that favorite object.

➤ Assure your child that he doesn't have to say or do anything he doesn't want to say or do.

➤ Tell your child that many children talk to counselors to help get over feeling anxious or shy.

➤ Remember to say encouraging words to your child like, "I know you can do it" or "If I were a counselor, I'd be looking forward to meeting a great kid like you."

The Sad Child

If your child is struggling with sad, hopeless, helpless feelings, he won't readily see the point in going to a counselor. This may be part of his depressive thinking. The idea of going to counseling won't inspire hope in him. He won't view it as an exciting prospect—and may even be irritable or claim he's too tired to talk to someone. Try to help your child invest in the idea, if even a tiny bit. Tell him that other children have actually felt as bad as he's feeling—or even worse—and that counseling has helped them. Express faith that things will be getting better, and be sure to tell him that he is worth the world to you—that you want him to feel better about life, about the future, and about himself. Sometimes sad or depressed children need to "borrow" some hope or optimism from an adult.

The Stressed Child

If your child is feeling highly stressed, he may be relieved to have an adult actually notice his stress and insist he talk about it with someone. Even so, he may have several reasons to resist counseling:

- He may not want to talk about whatever it is that he finds to be stressful because doing so makes him upset or emotionally uncomfortable. That's why children who've experienced divorce or a death, witnessed accidents, or been traumatized will hold back from talking because doing so creates the images and discomfort they're trying so hard to avoid.

- He may not want to talk for fear of burdening or hurting you— or some other significant person in his life. He might worry that talking will make matters worse somehow, either for others or for himself.

- He might have trouble making up his mind who he can trust, because stress and trauma has reduced his ability to trust.

Assure your stressed out child that it's not his fault; there's nothing wrong with him, and he didn't cause the stress (divorce, death, or trauma) in his life. Tell him that getting help is important, not because there's something wrong with him, but because he's been through a very hard time.

The Ashamed Child

While a slight sense of failure or shame is a common reaction if a child is struggling with behavioral or emotional problems, there are certain problems that are almost guaranteed to produce major embarrassment. Bed-wetting, loss of bowel control, eating problems, and sexual development problems are examples of very embarrassing or humiliating problems. If your child is dealing with such problems, taking a firm, but very gentle and reassuring stance will help. You might want to say something like this to your child: "I know you don't want to talk to a counselor about your pooping troubles, but I've found someone who works with lots and lots of kids who have your same problem. It's not that unusual, you know, and we haven't solved this ourselves. It's time to get help. *It's the same kind of help lots of other kids get.* And you know what? No one needs to know except you and me."

If you make that last statement, be sure you keep your promise of privacy. If you've already talked with family members or teachers, let the child know you've done so; don't pretend a level of privacy exists that isn't really there. Talking about your child's problems behind his back and without his permission can seriously damage the trust in your relationship. Be careful about sharing information about your child's embarrassing problems with anyone who may not keep it confidential.

No Surprises

It's never a good idea to trick children by not telling them you're taking them to see a professional and then just showing up at the office. On one occasion, a mother called me (Rita) to make an appointment for her son, explaining to me that she was very worried about her child's attitude and general energy level. The mother had heard rumors that her son was making very sad, depressed statements to his friends, and his usually excellent grades were slipping. I agreed to see the boy and made the appointment. The next week, when his mother brought him to the office, I went out to greet them and found one very angry child and a distraught mother. As it turned out, the child hadn't realized that his mother was taking him to see a counselor until he read the sign on our office door. As you might imagine, there was plenty of work to do before trust could be established!

You might assume it's better to let the counselor tell your child all about counseling. It's true that counselors can explain how counseling works, and give all sorts of details and encouragement, but you, as the parent, need to inform your child in advance about the counseling appointment. Even if you're feeling strung out and not very capable of telling your child about the decision to get help, it's important that he know ahead of time.

Reassure Your Child

Do your best to tell your child that you've made this decision, that you are making an appointment, and that you believe it will all come out for the better. Let him know the time and date of the appointment. Let him know where the professional's office is, how you chose that person, how long the session will last, and any other details that might make the child feel more in control. Your child may ask any number of funny, disarming, alarming, or accusing questions. Answer any questions your child has, and if you can't answer them, call the professional you've chosen, and ask how to respond. Below are a few examples of questions your child might have. Anticipating them, and thinking ahead about reassuring ways to respond, may help with your preparation.

- "Will I get a shot or have to take pills?"
- "Will I have to say things I don't want to say?"
- "Are you taking me there because I am bad?"
- "Do you think I'm crazy?"
- "Will they put me in the hospital for nut-cases?"
- "Why don't you see a shrink? You're the one with the problems."
- "If I promise to sleep alone and not cry anymore, can I stay home?"

You get the idea. Children need reassurance that they're neither bad nor crazy. They need reassurance that you'll be in this with them, and that you're willing to make changes, too.

Confidentiality

One question your child might ask, and one that's important to explore is: Will the counselor tell you everything I say? He may also wonder: Will the counselor tell my teacher? Grandma? Who will know? These are important questions. First, you and your child should understand that the counseling relationship is a private, confidential one, but there are certain things that professionals cannot keep private, at least in the United States. These things vary from state to state, and can be influenced by agency policies as well, so you need to ask the counselor very specifically about what can be kept confidential, and what cannot. Generally speaking, most states require counselors to disclose information about potentially dangerous situations (suicidal or homicidal impulses) or information about child abuse. This information has to be shared with state, county, or other government agencies that, in cases where risk for harm is high, may investigate the situation to insure the child's safety.

Besides the laws and policies that affect confidentiality, you also need to find out from the counselor—with your child present—what you, as parent, will be told and what the child can expect the counselor to keep private. Technically, you have access to your child's medical and mental health records up to a certain age, which again varies by state and topic area. However, professionals who work with children often develop policies that allow children and parents to come to an understanding about what level of detail is shared with the parents, and what can be kept just between the child and the counselor. It's important for everyone to understand how this will work. It can make a big difference in everyone's comfort level.

An Act of Love and Hope

Choosing to get help is not an easy decision. You may feel some uncertainty about making this choice, but when you do so, it's because your child matters so much to you. You want him to be happy and live well. Your decision to get help is a loving one.

It's also an important statement of faith in your child. Sometimes, children think parents are taking them to see a counselor because their parents have given up on them. Let your child know that the opposite is true, that going to counseling is a positive choice based on hope for positive change. If you take your child to see a counselor, it's because you believe things can get better, and your child is worth the trouble and cost of seeking this help. Assure your child that your choice to get professional help is not, in any way, an act of desperation or a punishment—instead, it's an act of hope.

Similarly, this book is an act of hope. We believe in parents. We believe most parents dearly love their children and want the very best for them. We believe in you. We also know that life may hand you many challenges.

We hope we've shown you that there's no need to feel embarrassed or inadequate for seeking professional help for your troubled child. Parenting wasn't meant to be a solo act. The heart of wise parenting, and wise living in general, is to get the right help at the right time from the right sources to accomplish what's needed. Thanks for loving your child enough to read this book. And thanks for getting your child the help he needs.

Check It Out

How to Help Children with Common Problems by Charles E. Schaefer and Howard L. Millman (Northvale, NJ: Jason Aronson, 1995). Many, if not most, common childhood behavioral problems are listed, with good case examples and helpful parenting suggestions.

Is My Child OK? When Behavior Is a Problem, When It's Not, and When to Seek Help by Henry A. Paul (New York: Random House, 2000). This book has a short-chapter, cookbook format that gives you descriptions and guidance on most problems children might display.

Appendix

Frequently Asked Questions

The following is a list of questions that parents frequently ask, or wish they could ask, when their child is having emotional or behavioral problems. We offer brief thoughts and guidance in response to the questions here, but you can find more help regarding these questions throughout this book.

Does my child's emotional problems mean I've blown it as a parent?

If you're reading this book and are willing to acknowledge your child may have problems, then you're definitely a caring parent who can still make a difference in your child's life. In fact, you've probably already done a lot more *right* than you give yourself credit for.

Still, it's normal to feel overwhelmed and disappointed in yourself if your child is struggling and you haven't been able to be as helpful as you want to be. Or perhaps you feel totally responsible for what's gone wrong—another common reaction. Please remember that children's problems arise from many complex and interrelated sources. Their genetic makeup; their school, social, and family environments; their personalities; the choices they make themselves; and sometimes their parents combine together to cause children's problems. Rarely is any one factor completely to blame—including you

If you feel like you've blown it, try not to get too wrapped up in your guilt. To be honest, we all blow it sometimes. We forget to listen when we should. We overreact to small matters. We come up with a consequence for a misbehavior that makes things worse. The point is that there's no such thing as the perfect parent because everyone makes mistakes.

Besides, the whole concept of "blowing it" suggests that you've given this parenting thing your best shot and it's somehow *over*. Of course, that's not true. Your parenting is a lifelong commitment. So rather than spending time blaming yourself, remember all the good things you've done and then set out to do the best you can for the rest of your life.

Isn't professional help only necessary for people who are really crazy, or mentally "sick"?

If that were the case then there must be lots of really crazy and mentally sick people out there, because lots of people—adults and children—are getting professional help. Actually, people don't have to be crazy or sick to need help. If your child is hurting and you're not sure what to do, getting help is a sign of intelligence; you're taking steps to address the problem before things get worse. Concerned parents with children who are already fairly healthy usually can improve their situation and condition remarkably quickly, which is rewarding for everyone involved.

Many people who seek and get help have very minor problems. Also, counseling is sometimes provided as a preventative measure. For instance, if your child has a traumatic experience or loses a loved one to death, having a chance to talk it out in a supportive group or individually with a professional can make it so your child never develops serious symptoms.

Is there a danger in giving my child's problem a medical label?

Generally speaking, accurate medical labels are a good thing. They explain what's been going on, help professionals communicate important information to one another, and point to the most effective interventions or treatments.

Unfortunately, sometimes medical labels can hurt. For example, your child may feel embarrassed about being "labeled" as depressed or hyperactive, or the label may cause teachers or other important adults to treat your child differently than others. On the other hand, a far greater danger is letting the fear of labeling keep you from getting needed professional help.

To limit the dangers of labeling, make sure you get help from a well-trained professional who will label your child accurately and confidentially, and will do so only after a thorough diagnostic work-up. As noted above, many people get professional help even though they don't have a diagnosable disorder. They simply have some problems in their life and want help getting through them.

Shouldn't we just handle childhood problems at home?

We always support home-based approaches to help children. That's why we've included helpful hints for you to use at home in every chapter in this book. Without a doubt, if you can handle the problems at home, it makes perfect sense to do so.

However, home-based approaches work best when combined with thoughtful reading or consultation with day care staff, school personnel, or mental health professionals. Most of the time, if your child has serious emotional or behavior problems, it's crucial to develop a home-professional partnership.

In other words, don't isolate yourself and your child from potential helpful information, input, or services. Do everything you can at home, but don't be afraid to reach out for professional help as well. As we say many times in this book, getting help when you need it is a sign of wisdom, not failure.

How can I be sure to get the right kind of help for my child?

This is a very important question. We encourage you to do some research. Read Chapter 11 in this book, talk to school personnel and other knowledgeable people in the community, and consider interviewing a few professionals. When deciding on a professional, look for excellent training and credentials, and a good personal fit. This takes investigating. Remember, you're the consumer—the person paying someone to do something for you. Therefore, you have the right to ask as many questions as you see fit. You also have the right to ask every professional you meet with about his or her educational background, experience, and past treatment successes.

How soon can I expect results if my child begins counseling? What if I don't see any results?

Sometimes you'll see results very quickly and sometimes it will seem like forever. Of course, the real answer to these questions is: "It depends." It depends on your child's unique problems, the particular treatment approach, and many other factors. Therefore, after you've chosen a professional, ask her or him when to expect results and what to do if results aren't happening. Experienced professionals will give you an idea about what timeline to expect.

Your mental health provider will want to know if you're seeing any positive or negative changes in your child. The key is to work hard on communicating effectively with your mental health provider. If you don't see any results within what you consider to be a reasonable time period, ask your friends, family, day care providers, school personnel, other professionals, or anyone you trust about whether your expectations are realistic. It's easy to become impatient when your child's well-being is at stake. Therefore, you should check in with others before you let your impatience cause you to stop whatever treatment you're getting.

How do I talk to my child about getting professional help?

Children are rarely thrilled about the idea of seeing a professional. We discuss approaches to dealing with your child's reluctance in Chapter 12, but the short answer is this: Talk in a hopeful, firm, loving manner that is nonaccusatory and especially, nonpunitive. The worst thing you can do is to have your child believe that going to counseling is a punishment. The next worst thing is to make your child feel as if she is crazy, defective, or mentally sick. Offer lots of reassurance about what a smart decision it is to get the help you need and that many really cool people go to counseling when they have life problems. You can also offer rewards for giving it a try, and you can offer other kinds of emotional support. In some situations, you can even offer to give the child a little more time to work out the problems herself, but only if you have a very clear timeline, and a way to measure progress.

How do I explain my child's problems to friends and relatives?

You need to decide, based on your unique personal situation, what exactly to tell your friends and family. Of course, the community around you is central to your emotional health and well-being. In many cases, family and friends will be helpful and understanding and will respect your choice to get professional help for your child's problems. On the other hand, sometimes, you may need to defend your decision. If you do, you may find this analogy helpful: If a child's teeth are decayed, crooked, and generally unhealthy, parents would be negligent if they decided to pull out the teeth themselves, or ignore the dental problems as they slowly worsened. Seeking the help of a trained dentist is essential, and can make a difference in the child's appearance, both in the present and in the future. The same goes for emotional and behavioral troubles. Parents can't be expected to know how to treat many of these problems. Simply trying to "pull them out" or ignore them is negligent, and won't work. In summary, explain the need for help, and express hope and confidence that, given the right intervention, things can get much better.

If I take my child for professional help, should I tell school personnel or others?

There's no need to announce to your mail delivery person or the soccer coach that your child is in counseling. In fact, for the most part, that information is private and talking about it too much can really embarrass or hurt your child. But it also isn't wise or necessary to act like it's a shameful secret. Sometimes, there will be good reasons to confide in adults who are important in your child's life. This depends on the problem areas, the reasons for counseling, and your child's feelings. If your child is seeking help for a temper problem which has flared a number of times during basketball team practice, telling the coach about the counseling might be helpful for everyone involved. Telling your child's teacher that he's getting counseling because of a trauma in his life might also be very useful information. Who to tell and when to tell them are good topics to talk over with your child's therapist, and with your child.

What should I do if people tease my child or make other inappropriate comments?

Most parents we know love their children so much that if someone makes intentionally hurtful remarks about one of their children, they may feel like literally slugging that someone or telling that person off. Our advice is: Don't do it!

It's very sad, but the human capacity for both unintentional and malice-filled hurtful interactions is boundless. As we've mentioned in the book, your child may be an easy target for teasing, labeling, or harsh judgments. If this occurs in public, your best first choice is probably to try educating the offending party. Tell the person that the comments are not necessary, not accurate, or not welcome. If a simple statement designed to educate this person doesn't work, your next best choice is to model for your child how to effectively deal with difficult people. Options include walking away, using humor, and contacting an authority (a parent, teacher, principal, or other appropriate adult).

During or after a teasing incident, it's helpful to talk with your child about her feelings when she's teased or asked about counseling. Remind her that people get teased for all sorts of positive efforts: Children whose parents make them practice piano get teased.

Children whose parents make them eat vegetables in front of other children get teased. Children also get teased for wearing glasses, making straight A's, and getting pimples. Point out to your child that the problem is really with the teaser, who is probably insecure and needs to tease others in order to feel important.

What if a professional gives my child a diagnosis after seeing him or her very briefly? And what if I don't agree with the diagnosis? What should I do?

Express your concerns directly to the professional. As consumers, you and your child deserve a professional who will be thoughtful and cautious about assigning diagnostic labels. If you have concerns, speak up. If you continue to have concerns or think your professional isn't listening, speak up some more. If you still don't feel satisfied, seek another professional opinion.

Index

A

Abnormal behavior, definition of, 3
Abrahams, George, 114
Activity level, as a dimension of
    temperament, 13
Acute stress disorder. *See* Trauma
Adaptability, as a dimension of
    temperament, 13
Adderholdt, Miriam, 43
ADHD. *See* Attention deficit hyperactivity
    disorder (ADHD)
Aggression. *See* Misconduct
Ahlbrand, Sheila, 114
Alcohol/drug abuse
    age and, 170, 171
    examining your own attitudes toward
        alcohol and drug use, 169–170
    getting professional help for, 173
    as the most likely problem your
        child will face, 170
    preventing, 171–172
    scenario illustrating, 170
    setting a "no use" rule, 171
    signs of a serious problem with, 172
American Academy of Child and
    Adolescent Psychiatry (Web site), 197
American Counseling Association
    (Web site), 197
American Psychological Association
    (Web site), 197
American School Counselor Association
    (Web site), 198
Anger. *See* Defiance/anger
Anger (Tavris), 146
Anorexia. *See* Eating difficulties
Anxieties. *See* Fears and anxieties
Approach, tendency to, as a dimension of
    temperament, 13
Armstrong, Thomas, 77
Arnold, Samuel J., 62
Asperger's Syndrome (Attwood), 174
Association for Advancement of Behavior
    Therapy (Web site), 198
Attachment parenting, 53–54
attachmentparenting.org, 63
Attention deficit hyperactivity
    disorder (ADHD)
    causes of, 70–71
    diagnosing, 66–68
    finding more information on, 77
    finding support for yourself, 76
    getting professional help for, 72–73
    helpful hints for, 75–76
    incidence of, in children, 64, 68
    inconsistent display of symptoms, 73–75
    intensifying *vs.* reducing symptoms, 71

    knowing when it's not, 69–70
    main features of, 66
    managing, 75
    medications for, 72, 73
    in new and stimulating situations, 74
    in one-on-one *vs.* group situations, 75
    scenarios illustrating, 64–65, 74
    signs of a serious problem with
        (hyperactive/impulsive type), 68
    signs of a serious problem with
        (predominately inattentive type), 67
    temperament and, 70
    types of, 66
Attention-Deficit/Hyperactivity Disorder (Silver), 77
Attention span, as a dimension
    of temperament, 14
Attwood, Tony, 174

B

Baby and Toddler Sleep Program (Pearce), 62
Barkley, Russell A., 77
Bedwetting. *See* Toileting troubles
*Behavioral Intervention for Young Children with
    Autism* (Maurice), 174
Behavioral therapies, 194
Bereavement, helping children with, 122, 131
Bettelheim, Bruno, 21
Beyer, Roberta, 131
Biddulph, Steve, 62
Bill of Rights for Children of Divorce, 124–125
Bipolar Child, The (Papolos), 94
Bipolar disorder. *See* Mania
Bladder problems. *See* Toileting troubles
Body problems
    body image and eating difficulties, 59–61
    body-mind connection, 46
    feelings of shame about, 44–45
    finding more information on, 62–63
    love-hate relationship with bodies, 44
    parental response to, 44
    scenarios illustrating, 45–46
    sleep problems, 53–58
    toileting troubles, 47–53
Bowel problems. *See* Toileting troubles
Boy v. Girl? (Abrahams), 114
Boy Who Couldn't Stop Washing, The
    (Rapoport), 174
Brainstorms (Horacek), 77
Breggin, Peter R., 77
Building the Bonds of Attachment (Hughes), 158
Bulimia. *See* Eating difficulties
Bullies Are a Pain in the Brain (Romain), 158
Buscaglia, Leo, 131

About the Authors

Drs. Rita Sommers-Flanagan and John Sommers-Flanagan are parents. Though they've had many other educational opportunities, parenting has been the most informative, profound, maddening, and rewarding. Their professional work as clinical psychologists, family consultants, and teachers has done nothing but deepen their appreciation of families, children, and the difficulties everyone faces as children grow and develop. Rita received her Ph.D. in clinical psychology in 1989 from the University of Montana and teaches there in counselor education. John received his Ph.D. in clinical psychology in 1986 from the University of Montana. He has been a college professor and a therapist, and he currently directs a nonprofit organization dedicated to parent education and support. John occasionally claims that receiving his degree three years ahead of Rita makes him the wiser of the two, but this remains a hotly contested claim.

Other Great Books from Free Spirit

Our Family Meeting Book
Fun and Easy Ways to Manage Time, Build Communication, and Share Responsibility Week by Week
by Elaine Hightower and Betsy Riley
Family meetings are proven ways to involve everyone in planning, solving problems, and staying close. This inviting book makes family meetings manageable, meaningful, and enjoyable for everyone. For parents. *$16.95; 136 pp.; softcover; color photos & illus.; lay-flat binding; 9" x 9"*

What Young Children Need to Succeed
Working Together to Build Assets from Birth to Age 11
by Jolene L. Roehlkepartain and Nancy Leffert, Ph.D.
Help create a firm foundation for children from day one. Here you'll find practical, concrete ways to build 40 assets in four different age groups. This friendly and easy-to-use book will make anyone an asset builder and a positive influence in children's lives. For parents, teachers, all other caring adults, and children. *$11.95; 320 pp.; softcover; illus.; 5¼" x 8"*

What Kids Need to Succeed
Proven, Practical Ways to Raise Good Kids
Revised, Expanded, and Updated Edition
by Peter L. Benson, Ph.D., Judy Galbraith, M.A., and Pamela Espeland
This book identifies 40 developmental "assets" kids need to lead healthy, productive lives, then gives them suggestions for building their own assets at home, at school, in the community, and in the congregation. *Parents' Choice* approved. For parents, teachers, community and youth leaders, and teens. *$5.99; 256 pp.; softcover; 4⅛" x 6⅞"*

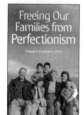

Freeing Our Families from Perfectionism
by Thomas S. Greenspon, Ph.D.
Perfectionism is not about doing our best. It's about believing that if we can just do something perfectly, other people will love and accept us—and if we can't, we'll never be good enough. In this encouraging, insightful book, Tom Greenspon explains perfectionism, where it comes from (including influences outside the family), and what to do about it. For parents. *$14.95; 128 pp.; softcover; illust.; 6" x 9"*

The Survival Guide for Parents of Gifted Kids
How to Understand, Live With, and Stick Up for Your Gifted Child
Revised & Updated Edition
by Sally Yahnke Walker
Up-to-date information about giftedness, gifted education, problems, personality traits, and more, written by an educator of gifted kids and their parents. For parents of children ages 5 & up.
$14.95; 152 pp.; softcover; illus.; 6" x 9"

To place an order or to request a free catalog of SELF-HELP FOR KIDS® and SELF-HELP FOR TEENS® materials, please write, call, email, or visit our Web site:

Free Spirit Publishing Inc.
217 Fifth Avenue North • Suite 200 • Minneapolis, MN 55401-1299
toll-free 800.735.7323 • local 612.338.2068 • fax 612.337.5050
help4kids@freespirit.com • www.freespirit.com

Visit us on the Web!

www.freespirit.com

Stop by anytime to find our Parents' Choice Approved catalog with fast, easy, secure 24-hour online ordering; "Ask Our Authors," where visitors ask questions—and authors give answers—on topics important to children, teens, parents, teachers, and others who care about kids; links to other Web sites we know and recommend; fun stuff for everyone, including quick tips and strategies from our books; and much more! Plus our site is completely searchable so you can find what you need in a hurry. Stop in and let us know what you think!

Just point and click!

 Get the first look at our books, catch the latest news from Free Spirit, and check out our site's newest features.

 Do you have a question for us or for one of our authors? Send us an email. Whenever possible, you'll receive a response within 48 hours.

order! Order in confidence! Our secure server uses the most sophisticated online ordering technology available. And ordering online is just one of the ways to purchase our books: you can also order by phone, fax, or regular mail. No matter which method you choose, excellent service is our goal.

1.800.735.7323 • fax 612.337.5050 • help4kids@freespirit.com

If you liked **PROBLEM CHILD OR QUIRKY KID?**, you'll also like
OUR FAMILY MEETING BOOK and WHAT YOUNG CHILDREN NEED TO SUCCEED

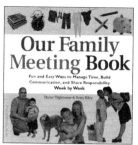

1-57542-120-8, $16.95

OUR FAMILY MEETING BOOK

Fun and Easy Ways to Manage Time, Build Communication, and Share Responsibility

This colorful step-by-step guide helps busy families organize, prioritize, strengthen ties, and otherwise keep it together.

1-57542-070-8, $11.95

WHAT YOUNG CHILDREN NEED TO SUCCEED

Working Together to Build Assets from Birth to Age 11

Learn how to build developmental assets—family support, positive values, social skills, and more. Includes over 1,000 tips and activities.

Call **1.800.735.7323** to order anytime or mail this card for a FREE catalog!

Send me a Free Spirit catalog!

name (please print) _____

street _____

city/state/zip _____

email _____

Order online at ***www.freespirit.com*** and download excerpts, quizzes, and more!

Want to know more about **MAKING POSITIVE CHOICES, COPING WITH CHALLENGES, KEEPING IT TOGETHER,** and **MAKING A DIFFERENCE?**

Free Spirit can help! We're the award-winning source of SELF-HELP FOR KIDS® and SELF-HELP FOR TEENS®. We know the issues young people face, and we have the information and tips you need to succeed. Mail this card for a FREE catalog. (And have one sent to a friend!)

Send me a Free Spirit catalog!

name (please print) _____

street _____

city/state/zip _____

email _____

Send one to my friend: (A ❏ teacher ❏ parent ❏ youth worker)

name (please print) _____

street _____

city/state/zip _____

email _____

Order online at ***www.freespirit.com*** and download excerpts, quizzes, and more!

Our Family Meeting Book

Two busy moms share the cure for over-scheduled families.

BUSINESS REPLY MAIL

FIRST-CLASS MAIL   PERMIT NO. 26589   MINNEAPOLIS MN

POSTAGE WILL BE PAID BY ADDRESSEE

free spirit PUBLiSHiNG®
217 Fifth Avenue North, Suite 200
Minneapolis, MN 55401-9776

Free Spirit Publishing
Your SELF-HELP FOR KIDS®
and SELF-HELP FOR TEENS®
source for 20 years.

BUSINESS REPLY MAIL

FIRST-CLASS MAIL   PERMIT NO. 26589   MINNEAPOLIS MN

POSTAGE WILL BE PAID BY ADDRESSEE

free spirit PUBLiSHiNG®
217 Fifth Avenue North, Suite 200
Minneapolis, MN 55401-9776